Youth Specialties

How Intentional Activity Can
Make the Spiritual Stuff Stick

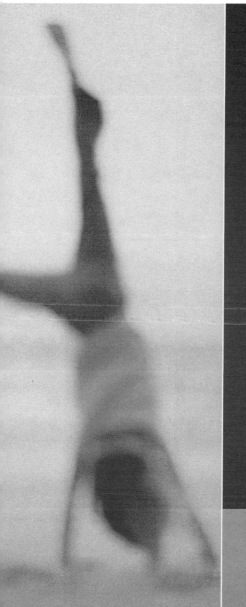

Experiential
Youth
Ministry
Handbook

JOHN**LOSEY**

Youth Specialties

Experiential Youth Ministry Handbook: How Intentional Activity Can Make the Spiritual Stuff Stick
Copyright © 2004 by Youth Specialties

Youth Specialties Books, 300 South Pierce Street, El Cajon, CA 92020, are published by Zondervan,
5300 Patterson Avenue SE, Grand Rapids, MI 49530

Library of Congress Cataloging-in-Publication Data

Losey, John, 1965-
  Experiential youth ministry handbook : how intentional activity can
make the spiritual stuff stick / by John Losey.
      p. cm.
Includes bibliographical references.
  ISBN 0-310-25532-5 (pbk.)
  1. Church work with youth. I. Title.
BV4447 .L66 2004
259'.23--dc22

2003025493

Editing by Vicki Newby
Cover and interior design by Rule29
Printed in the United States of America

04 05 06 07 08 09 / DC / 10 9 8 7 6 5 4 3 2

Experiential Youth Ministry Handbook
How Intentional Activity Can Make the Spiritual Stuff Stick

Dedication

This book is for those who have the
"Dangerous Wonder" that leads them
on amazing adventures in life as well
as in ministry.

In the spirit of Yac!

Acknowledgments

Thanks to:

All the kids, camps, corporations, churches, campuses, and conference centers[a] I've worked with. I've learned something from all of you.

My family, especially my parents, Jim and Sally. Thanks for all the good counsel, advice, and support.[b]

The great group of people I've worked with at W.I.L.D, OLE, IV, and Praxis.

Jeff Tacklind and Lars Rood for continuing to challenge me with their own views on experiential stuff.

Tom Leahy, Jim Cain, Lisa Blockus, Chris Cavert, Dick Hammond, Dave Vermilye, and the rest of the talented facilitators I've met through NCCPS.

Joe and Beth Slevcove for the great questions, conversations, and support.

The YS people—Marko for an amazing 2.5 year conversation that resulted in this book, Dave Urbanski for enduring my questions.[c]

Vicki Newby, my very patent editor. Thank you for helping me sound coherent and for asking all the right questions.

The people at Diedrich's Coffee House on 17th Street in Costa Mesa where I wrote about 80 percent of this book.

[a] Too much alliteration?

[b] Even when I didn't take your good counsel and advice.

[c] Some good questions, some not so much.

Contents

Introduction

A good question is better than a weak answer.
"Good enough" seldom is.

Good questions lead us on. Questions drive a story and keep it moving. Two questions drive the story of this book:

• How do people learn and grow?
• How can we as leaders and teachers best help others in that process?

The story of this book is about the *quest*[1] for the answers, not the answers themselves. Much of my quest has been in the context of working with youth. Youth ministry raised many great questions.[2] Too often, instead of living with the question, I would focus on finding a quick answer. As long as my story focused on finding answers, I found my teaching and leading was about informing people. "Let me give you the answers."

As my focus shifted to the questions themselves, my teaching and leading moved from a desire to inform to a passion to *transform*. I discovered that when I offer my own path to the answer, I often cheat people out of the journey to find their own answers. Any answer tends to stop people from pursuing their own process of discovery. Focusing on the questions leads us to create opportunities for people to discover their own stories.

A good question leads people on an adventure of their own. As they journey, they create their own story and will own the breakthroughs and discoveries. Once we arrive at an answer, our desire to seek more answers disappears. But the question leads to transformation.

This turning point in the story of this book created a new way for me to go about providing materials for training. It has also impacted the content and thought behind this book. Instead of providing a document that attempts to predict and address every question and situation, I offer a simple skeleton on which you can hang your experience. Models and methods become starting points you can modify, rewrite, and make your own.

With experience and training comes authority and the wisdom to apply and modify methods to make them your own. Books like this let you borrow the authority of an expert to take advantage of their training and experience. I encourage you

[1] After all, *quest* is related to *question*.

[2] How can I present the gospel in an exciting, practical way? Why do students show up for some events and not others? How do you get Silly Putty out of carpet?

to borrow the authority I've accumulated through my successes and failures. But you may only *borrow* it.

As you try out these ideas, you'll gain your own experience. As you succeed and fail and wrestle with these concepts, you'll gain your own authority. My stories can serve you only for so long. You'll find your own voice, your own perspective. You'll release the authority you borrowed from me to find your own.

As you picked up this book, I hope you acknowledged the inherent irony of a book about intentional experience.[3] For the most part books and reading are passive, not interactive. Most books, especially resource books, stay external. Books are easy to keep at arm's length so they never enter into our hearts and transform our lives from the inside out. They remain distant objects for evaluation and analysis. We keep them on the shelf until we need a diversion or an idea. The book stays out only long enough for us to capture the content or steal on idea.

Experience is an exchange, a relationship. It's mine as much as I'm its. I become about it as much as it's about me. To qualify as experience, I must be engaged and interacting with the moment. We enter into experience. Rarely has a book, even classic fiction, pulled me into it.[4]

I would love for you to not just read this book but experience it. Enjoy the irony of the situation and interact with the content. Consider this a formal invitation to make this book about you. Use this book for your own ends. Talk to it as you read. Write in the margins. Underline, cross out, highlight, scribble over the words. Redraw the diagrams. Doodle on the pictures. Use this book as a hockey puck or as kindling for a fire. Create some sort of conversation with this book.[5] Let this book impact you, and allow yourself to impact this book.

You probably have already noticed the footnotes.[6] I've made an intentional attempt to encourage you to interact with this material. I'm using the footnotes as a device to let you peek into the conversation I'm having with the material.[7] Most of the comments will be directly related to the material. Some footnotes will hint at other topics or areas of future inquiry. Some footnotes take potshots at the material in an attempt to preempt sarcastic comments that may pass through your mind as you read.

I hope that, between the content of the text and content of the footnotes, you'll gain insight into my internal dialogue and my mental conflict as I've wrestled with this subject matter. I hope it reveals some of my own cynicism surrounding this material. It may even provide a bit of comic relief. My ultimate goal for the footnotes is to invite you, as a reader, into the conversation. Lend your voice, your ideas, and your experience to the dialogue so that we, together, can take these ideas further.

"How?" you may be asking yourself.[8] Read with a pen. Create your own footnotes as they occur to you. If a passage confuses you or raises a question, take a moment to identify it and write it in the margin. If a specific phrase or point causes a strong reaction, circle it or underline it. Describe your reaction in the margin. If something seems ridiculous to you, write down your thoughts. The footnotes are present not just for entertainment but to serve as a model for you to read this book experientially.

This has been a difficult project for me. I'm not overly fond of games books.[9] It's

---

[3] In the past I mocked the fact that *Experiencing God* was published in a workbook format. I thought filling in the blanks was far from experiencing the presence of God. Now for integrity's sake, I must either express my regret at the mocking or include this project in the mockery.

[4] I can count on one hand the books that I can say I experienced. I can point to the tear stains on my copy of *Where the Red Fern Grows*.

[5] Yes, I have found myself talking to a book as I read in public. It can be embarrassing at first, but the strange looks you get can be entertaining.

[6] I hope you have.

[7] I realize this is a conversation with myself. But remember I also talk to books.

[8] Look! You're already asking yourself questions.

[9] To say that I *hate* games books may be overly dramatic but *intense* dislike is too many syllables and sounds wimpy.

not that I can't see the usefulness of reference books. It's just that there's an addictive quality to them that can discourage growth and depth. Once all the games have been played, then what do you do? Look for the next book. Hooked on the ease and convenience of having an expert think for us, we become resource junkies. "Dude, can you score me another set of conversation starters?"[10]

This book finds its best use in the hands of youth workers who have no training in this area and no one to train them. They need to borrow authority from somewhere.[11] A resource book feels to them like a life preserver feels to a drowning person or a security blanket feels to a frightened child.

After this point, resource books get scary. They become like cookbooks, and our ministries become recipe driven. When I need a new lesson, I pull the cookbook off the shelf and—ta da!—instant success. It's so easy and takes so little time and energy. Why wouldn't we? Why shouldn't we?

The recipe approach offers a seductive solution to the problem of programming. Ministry is hard work. It takes time and energy to accomplish all we're called to. Most youth workers are overworked and underpaid—and many end up burned out and used up. Why not take advantage of easy ways to prepare lessons?

Because easy doesn't make it right. In fact, this approach may be making the problem worse. If my life is moving too fast, I don't need something that makes it move faster. If I'm too busy to plan a lesson, I may be too busy.[12]

When we depend on games, books or curriculum, we depend on others to wrestle with the issues for us. We don't grapple with the subject or the methods ourselves. With little personal investment, we end up disconnected. If we're not connected to our own program, how can we expect the staff or students to be?

As we wrestle with the subject matter and program components, we become intimately connected to them—which creates passion and depth. Students know when you're passionate and connected to the program and respond by pressing further and deeper into their own journeys. The wrestling to reach this depth and passion consumes time and energy. It also encourages our growth toward God.

How to Use This Book

As I write this book, I have a mental picture of how it can and should be used. The problem is that once it's published, I've given up control of the application. You paid your money. Now you can use it any way you choose. Before you dive in, I want to give you an idea of how I see this book being used.[13]

The first section, Foundations, offers a look at basic experiential methods and how teachers and leaders in the Bible used them. This gives you a context and foundation for the rest of the book. I may use some words that are new to you, words like *praxis*, *initiative activity*, and *learning loop*. These words are intended to connect to your experiences and help you understand them better. If the new words help you, please use them. If you have other terms or phrases that make more sense to you, cross out my words and replace them with yours. There's nothing new under the sun.[14] My goal isn't to provide the latest, greatest, or the cutting edge. My desire is for us to connect our staff, our students, and ourselves to God and the life he's given us.

[10] Picture a scrubby-looking youth worker sitting outside a Christian bookstore with a hand-lettered sign that reads, "Will work for games book."

[11] This makes me think of "Guitar Shopping," a song by David Wilcox. If you've never heard of David Wilcox, I highly recommend sampling some of his material.

[12] I offer this as a thought to ponder, not as an accusation.

[13] Uh oh! My control issues are showing.

[14] I accept the cynicism of Ecclesiastes 1:9-10.

The second section, Activities and Exercises, offers a collection of experiential activities for you to use in your ministry. I've included initiatives, large and small group activities, and planning exercises. I've supplied you with brief descriptions of the activities, lists of equipment you'll need, issues to consider, safety issues, and variations, all so you can try them immediately.

The third section of this book, Program Templates, presents frameworks for common contexts found in youth ministry. These templates will help you plan programs and events in a way that experiential methods become a practical part of your ministry. Each template offers a planning strategy to follow for powerfully implementing the activities presented in the second section.

The appendixes contain sample programs—created by using the templates in the third section—along with other resources I recommend. Try the sample programs and explore the resources. Get a feel for how they work. Take some time to let the experiences impact you. (You'll be amazed at the results when you give time to reflection.) After reflecting, tweak the programs and templates to work even better.

As you make connections between what works and why, you'll also move toward a deeper understanding of how your students learn and grow. You'll also find that you're growing into a deeper understanding of your own strengths and weaknesses and your unique contribution to the lives of your staff, students, and community. And that's the point: use this book, tweak it, change it, and make it your own.

Enjoy!

Section One

Foundations

Experiential Basics

One great thing about youth ministry is variety. You might be a small group leader for a church or you might be a camp counselor. One minute you're tossing jellybeans onto a face covered with whip cream, and the next you're praying alongside a hurting kid.

I'm fortunate to have worked in several kinds of ministries. I've spent many summers at camp, including a few at Indian Village, a rustic facility that's part of Forest Home Christian Conference Center. The campers slept in tepees, ate outside, and hiked a lot. They knew the staff members by their Indian names; I was Bear.

During my first summer at the Village, I was a lead counselor, meaning I led about 35 kids and five to seven counselors for a week. Armed with a backpack and leather vest, I taught kids about Jesus, led them in singing, taught them outdoor skills, and guided them on hikes.

The hikes especially were hot and dusty.[15] I often shed my vest and backpack and found a willing camper to lug them around for me. The kids were surprisingly excited to carry the heavy backpack or to wear the thick leather vest. They were happy. I was cooler. A classic win-win situation.

Several years later I was the Indian Village director. While interviewing potential staff members for the coming summer, I spoke to a guy who had been a camper in my tribe during my early years. He told me that I had a huge impact on his life. I asked if the impact was because of a Bible lesson I had taught or if it had been a worship time I led.

He shook his head. "Nope. It was the time you let me carry your backpack." He must have seen the confusion on my face as he continued. "I was blown away that you trusted me enough to carry your backpack. You thought I was responsible, and nobody had ever trusted me like that before."

As he explained how this act—significant to him, insignificant to me—started him on a new life path, I could think only about how giving up the pack was not about his growth but my comfort. He wasn't supposed to be learning then, was he?

The Bible studies, worship times, and evening meetings we put so much effort

[15] The only way you could tell the difference between the dirt on your skin and the tan is if it streaked when the sweat ran down.

into are supposed to be what touch lives. Yet for this camper, the most significant impact came from the real-life experience of carrying a backpack.

While the traditional teaching times play an important role in ministry, I've found that the most powerful lessons occur during real-life interactions. In all the ministry I've done, either working with students or training staff, experience has always been the best teacher. Whether accidental or intentional, experiences touch lives deeply.

In the case of this camper-turned-staff-applicant, my accidental lesson was powerfully positive. I shudder to think of all the accidental lessons I passed along that were significantly less encouraging.

There are no throwaway moments in youth ministry. Not only is someone always watching us, someone is always learning. Accidental experiences, like the boy with my backpack, do not always result in positive lessons. There is potential to learn something from every experience, but the lesson may not be helpful, especially if we aren't paying attention. But if we know that experience teaches and if we learn how to use experience intentionally, our ministries will touch lives in deep, positive ways.

Experiential methods intentionally use experience to transform lives. This approach to ministry utilizes events from life and from programmed encounters to teach, increase depth, and strengthen communities.

When you read the phrase *experiential methods*, you may conjure images of a small group of dirty, sweaty backpackers slogging along a mountain trail. Or maybe you envision a person perched on top of an 80-foot telephone pole, building up the courage to leap for a trapeze bar. If you're familiar with experiential methods at all, it's probably in the context of outdoor and adventure programming, two powerful applications of these methods. Group bonding and positive self-image are two common outcomes of this application.

Understanding how experiential methods work can help you move it from mountains to meeting rooms. Biblical truth can be brought to life by creating programs based on these methods. A basic understanding of the following models will help you better understand and apply the activities and programs presented later in this book.[16]

But be warned. These methods commonly produce extreme results. Lives will be transformed permanently and continuously. Providing information will never be enough for you anymore.

Praxis

Praxis is a little word that packs a big punch. It's an old word that's finding new life in the world of theology and in education.[17] Some have used it as a fancy way of saying, "Learn by doing." Others have given it more depth by describing it as the movement from theory to practice.

There's more to it really. Praxis is a way of understanding the world when, through reflection, what you do impacts how you think and how you think impacts what you do. It's the ongoing collision of theory, action, and reflection.[18]

[16] All models are descriptive but not necessarily prescriptive. What do I mean by that? Many models and theories attempt to describe what really happens but don't really try to deal with what should happen. A model is a lens to look through. Like a pair of glasses, models try to bring clarity to something that's fuzzy. It's an attempt to understand reality, but it's not reality itself. Models are only helpful if they bring clarity. When a model doesn't help us understand a situation, we need to let go of that model. Some people make the mistake of trying to force reality to fit a model even if it doesn't. Reading this footnote will pay off later in this chapter.

[17] Use it properly in a sentence and impress your seminary friends.

[18] My apologies to the practical theologians who might pick up this book. People who are much smarter than I am, with difficult-to-pronounce German names, have spent their lives studying and writing about this topic. This section on Praxis comes nowhere near addressing the deep, rich complexities that are revealed with further study. My understanding of Praxis has been influenced by the writings of James Fowler and Paulo Freire and through conversations with Dr. Amy Jacober (Seattle Pacific University) and Dr. Gordon Coulter (Azusa Pacific University).

Understanding the components and dynamics of Praxis can help you improve your current programs and can help you intentionally design new ones. The insights gained through this theory will benefit staff and students alike.

Praxis has three parts: theory, action, and reflection. While theory, action, and reflection can stand alone as important parts of programming, in Praxis these three connect, interact, and impact each other. Let's look at these parts separately first to make it easier to understand the dynamics between them.

Theory

Schools, seminaries, and other training opportunities are based on a particular theory or model.[19] They lay out a perspective on why and how things work. Theories are important because they express a collective memory on specific topics.

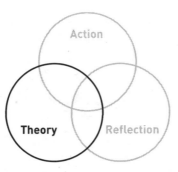

Figure 1-1
Praxis: Theory

> *"If I see any farther, it is because I stand on the shoulders of giants."*
>
> —ABRAHAM LINCOLN

They are the "shoulders of giants" that Abraham Lincoln stood upon to see farther. Because of theories and models, we don't reinvent the wheel or rediscover fire every generation. Hard-won lessons are passed on as an inheritance from those who preceded us, so we can move further along, add to our collective understanding, and pass new ideas on to those who come after us.

The desire to be innovative—on the cutting edge—sometimes lures us away from existing models and theories. But being creative doesn't mean we must ignore ideas that have worked.[20]

Another mistake is to place too much emphasis on a theory or model. The purpose-driven model, the seeker-sensitive model, and this experiential model are powerful, but they're created in a specific context and written in generalities. They can't be copied elsewhere and produce the same results. Students are different, the community is different, and you are different. Theories and models can't be ignored, nor are they the total solution. Theories must be considered along with who they'll be applied to and how they'll be acted on.

Theory makes up most of the content of formal education. It's easy to package, and the diagrams are interesting. From the teacher's standpoint, theory is tidy. Schools have limited time to get through mounds of material. Nice, neat models make packaging this material efficient and create great opportunities to pass along the collective wisdom born from the experience of those who have gone before.

> *"Ideas are poor ghosts until they become incarnate in a soul. Then they reach out and touch the world and shake it with a passion."*
>
> —GEORGE ELIOT

Theory must be applied to real life to be of value to us on the front lines of youth ministry. But real life is seldom as well defined as the theories and models we're

[19] This book, for instance, is based on the theory of experiential learning and provides models of how it works.

[20] Or even good ideas that didn't work.

given. Real life is messy.

Action

Many of us who are attracted to youth ministry find talking about theory boring— and maybe a waste of time. Talking about action is a different matter.

"Tell me what to do, so I can *do* ministry."

Ministry skills give us a head start in performing ministry. If you have little experience, these elements are vital. Giving staff specific assignments or students a step-by-step guide results in immediate and practical action. What we *do* is what touches the people we serve. Without action nothing gets accomplished.

Tips, tricks, and techniques make up the majority of content in training seminars. When youth workers spend their limited time and money on seminars, they want to walk away with hands-on skills they can use immediately. "Ten Steps to Effective Ministry" creates the instant gratification they seek.

The same principle is true for many sermons. Passing along specific actions can be neatly packaged in a workshop or sermon format. Limited time leads to training that cuts content to the bare essentials. "Just tell me what to do!" Learning the skills necessary for leading an activity, creating a lesson, or disciplining students is essential in becoming an effective youth worker just as learning how to pray is essential for being a Christian.

These skills are not just recipes for effectiveness. They're based on theory. There are reasons they work. Knowing the tricks will help in a specific context, but knowing why tricks work helps you transfer them to other situations. Actions that work in one situation may not be effective in another. Without direction, action may be wasted energy or chaos. The wrong action at the wrong time may cause damage to the people we're trying to build up.

Figure 1-2
Praxis: Action

> *Actions are mere convulsions until they become informed by thought and intent. Then they not only touch the world but also gently caress it.*
>
> —BEAR

We're all different, with unique personalities and talents. Certain skills required for ministry or spiritual disciplines come easier to some than others. A ministry may adopt a ministry model that requires a specific set of skills. Considering the *why* and *how* of ministry aren't enough. The *who* matters too. The people who will actually be living out the ministry—the students, leaders, and volunteers—must also be considered. If we're forced into a certain course of action that doesn't match who we are, we'll run away or burn out.

Reflection

So what's reflection? Reflection allows the space and time for an experience to impact people. Students and staff members personalize the teaching so it directly transforms their lives. Reflection is that moment that lets them breathe deep and consider how their lives might be impacted and changed by the new experience. It's that simple.

The difficult, scary part is trusting the silence and open space, having faith that reflection is effective. In the constant hustle of our culture, reflection seems like a waste of time. While people are reflecting, we receive few, if any, indications of what's going on inside them. We're tempted to fill the apparent void with more action or to move to the next concept. Fear of the void keeps us bouncing from topic to topic, from activity to activity, never allowing any of them to sink in. The result is that we know a lot but can't apply any of it. Can ministries function without reflection? Sure they can, but they're missing out on huge potential for depth and power.

"I've got to empty out the inside of my head."

—DAVID WILCOX

David: Reflection Illustrated

David and Saul were both anointed kings of Israel. God's blessing was taken from Saul, but David is known as a man after God's own heart. What made the difference?[21]

Saul did some terrible things as king. He took credit for what Jonathan did (1 Samuel 13:3), became jealous of David (1 Samuel 8:8), and killed 85 priests (1 Samuel 22:18), just to name a few. The turning point for Saul was when God told him to completely destroy the Amalekites. Saul won the battle, but he selected the best stuff to take home and sacrifice to God (1 Samuel 15:1-26). If we didn't hear God's command to Saul, his actions would seem to be great devotion to God. They weren't. By disobeying God, Saul made the victory about himself, not God. So God removed his blessing from Saul and had Samuel anoint David as king.

David also did some terrible things. He lied to protect himself (1 Samuel 21:2), murdered Uriah (2 Samuel 11:14-15), and had an affair with Bathsheba (2 Samuel 11:1-5).

How was David different from Saul?

David sat!

David finished with the battles and settled into his palace. There, he thought that God deserved to live in something better than a tent.[22,23] This seemed like a great idea to everyone including Nathan, David's pastor. But God had different plans. God told Nathan to pass along the message that David was not to build the temple.

At this point in the story, David was in the same situation as Saul. From the viewpoint of everyone on the outside, building the temple would have seemed like a great sacrifice to God. But David knew it was not God's desire. Building the temple would boost David's reputation as a man of God in everyone's eyes but God's. Instead of taking action, he reflected. He went to the tabernacle and sat before God.

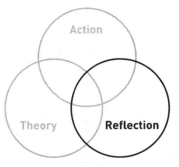

Figure 1-3
Praxis: Reflection

[21] Eugene Peterson's book *Leap Over a Wall* takes a refreshing look at the life of David and inspired this section.

[22] The full story is found in 1 Chronicles 17.

[23] The tabernacle was a portable tent used as God's house. God didn't really even want to move out of the tent. God liked to camp.

This moment of "inaction" is what set him apart from Saul. Reflection made the difference between being a common king and being a man after God's own heart.

You can function in ministry knowing what to do, how to do it, and why. But is that enough? Reflection connects ministry to who you are. Instead of following someone else's recipe, you're following *your* passion. Reflection encourages you to see how your life fits a theory and how your heart connects to your actions.

Dynamics

Theory, action, and reflection are important concepts by themselves, but separately, their power to transform is limited. Praxis finds its power in their interdependence. One or two of them aren't nearly as powerful as all three of them combined.

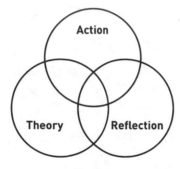

Figure 1-4
Praxis: Theory, Action, and Reflection

Have you ever used a projection TV? Many of them use three different lenses to project all the colors. Using only one of the lenses let's you see a pale, monochromatic image. You can barely make out an image on the screen. With two of the three lenses, you can see the motion better, but the images are strangely colored ghosts, off-color and far from the maker's intention. Only when all three lenses are projecting do the images appear in full color and intensity.

Theory, action, and reflection are the three lenses of Praxis. If one of them is missing, the entire image is distorted. Theory needs action to make it practical and reflection to make it personal. Action needs theory to give it direction and reflection to give it compassion. Reflection needs theory to give it content and action to give it application. When theory, action, and reflection interact, the result is a powerful learning environment in which lives are transformed.

Applications

How does understanding Praxis make your ministry better? If you read an earlier footnote, you'll remember that a model or theory is like a lens.[24] You look through it to see if it makes the topic clearer. Assess your ministry using Praxis as the lens. Are you familiar with the variety of ministry models and theories of ministry? Have you selected one purposefully? Are you keeping up with the latest media developments and recreation trends so they can be used appropriately? Are you giving students and staff time and space to wrestle with their calling and encouraging them to own it?

You'll find Praxis applied in a step-by-step process on page 23.[25]

The Amazing Learning Loop of Depth

"We had the experience but missed the meaning."

—T. S. ELIOT

One of the guiding questions of this book is, "How do people learn and grow?" If we can grasp this, we can be more intentional about helping people learn and grow. The

[24] If you haven't heard this before look back at the second footnote of this chapter. It pays to read the footnotes.

[25] You may want to review that information now.

Amazing Learning Loop of Depth is a model that gives us a practical sequence of events that build on each other.[26]

Using this model, we take a bit of information, encourage application, create a space for reflection, and finally re-view the experience to gain new insights.[27] The parts of the learning loop build on each other and also encourage ongoing learning, because each loop leads into the next. The steps may be the same each time through the loop, but they're processed on a different, deeper level. The topic may even be the same, but with each loop comes new dimensions to be explored.

Let's walk through the learning loop process. The loop can start at any of these steps, but we'll begin with *inform*. In the learning loop, *inform* is the content of a lesson or some other input. It might be a new skill, attitude, or perspective.

The next step is *apply*. The new information received at the *inform* step needs to be applied if it's ever going to impact the individual or the world. The information is tried out to see how it works. A skill is practiced or an attitude or perspective is tried on.

Once the information has been applied, it is important to create space for the next step—*reflect*. Allow the whole experience to sink in.

The space to reflect will improve the quality of the next step, *re-view* the process so far. What worked? What didn't? Did this information work when it was lived out? Re-viewing refines the information based on personal experience, which creates new information to try out. The learning loop is back to *inform*, and that new information needs to be applied, reflected on, and re-viewed so that more new information is produced.

Let's take a closer look at each of these steps.

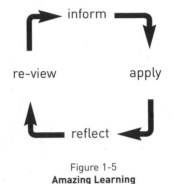

Figure 1-5
**Amazing Learning
Loop of Depth – top view**

Inform

The information step is the most familiar part of the loop, the traditional lesson time. The Bible study, the sermon, or the classroom lecture are all times when new information is presented. Theories, models, and concepts are laid out for us to consider. The talented teacher uses this opportunity to pass along skills that help us live better lives. The gifted speaker helps us see the possibility that we can be different.

This information is important, but it's only the first step. Being informed is not the same as being transformed. Many programs stop here. The assumption is that if the students have been told, the teacher's responsibility is finished. But more is needed. Information needs to be acted on or the information is trivia.

Apply

Giving students an opportunity to apply the information you have given them is what will lift the information out of the realm of trivia. This step in the learning loop impacts the world around us and touches the individual in a deeper way. Encouraging students to be doers of the Word is important, but we can help them succeed in this by providing a safe place to try out new behaviors and attitudes.

Connecting recreation activities to the teaching time is a great way to start the

[26] This is a variation of the experiential learning cycle developed by Kolb, Lewin, and Hahn. Creative credit goes to them and any blame for misuse is mine. The *learning loop* fits well and allows me to use words like *loopiness*. Conversations with Dr. Amy Jacober (Seattle Pacific University) gave me a better overall understanding of this process and an understanding of its connection to practical theology.

[27] I use the hyphen in *re-view* intentionally. I am emphasizing the concept of looking over the experience with a new perspective rather than just reminiscing.

learning loop. Recreation as application helps students realize that what they learn needs to impact how they live. Beginning the application in a safe, structured environment builds confidence as well.

You can try on new information like trying on shoes. You put on a new behavior or attitude and lace it up. To see how it fits, you wiggle around a bit, take a few steps, and maybe even run around. You may try on several pairs of shoes before you find the ones that fit well and don't give you blisters. You may be so excited about your new purchase that you put the old behavior in the new box and wear the new one out into the world.[28] Application time allows students to try on behaviors and attitudes while discovering what works and what doesn't, so that eventually they can live out the new information in a powerfully practical way.

Taking action on what you hear gives hands and feet to the information. It creates flesh and bones from the poor ghosts of ideas. Without another component though, this behavior is just imitation, like a parrot repeating phrases without knowing the meaning of the words. We can have a powerful experience and never grasp its meaning. The application may touch the world, but it never touches the person. There needs to be another step that encourages students to internalize the applications so that they touch their souls and transform their lives.

Reflect

The next two steps in the learning loop take learning to a transformational level. Providing an opportunity to reflect on the application of information is essential to accessing it at a deeper level. This is a simple yet fearful step to take. From the outside it looks like nothing is happening. Reflection is often dismissed as wasted time. Youth ministry is an action-oriented culture so we often overlook—or intentionally avoid—the reflection step.

Fear comes from the lack of control that is inherent in true reflection. Creating an open space for students to reflect means that youth leaders must let go of what they've taught and allow students to wrestle with it and come to their own conclusions about how their lives should be changed.

Allowing opportunities for reflection requires faith that God is truly in control of the learning. Reflection gives the Holy Spirit an opening to touch the lives of students. Reflection also encourages students to develop relationships with God independent of their relationships with youth pastors and peer groups. The faith required of the youth leader in this step creates an opportunity for God to reveal his power and faithfulness to the leaders as well as the students.

Reflection is learned. It comes easier to some than others, but everyone needs encouragement to reflect.

While reflection requires leaders to give up control, they still have a role in this step of the learning loop. It's possible to create a structure for reflecting without controlling it, but it's like holding a baby bird in your hands.[29] As it flutters around, you're tempted to tighten your grip to control the motion. But if you hold too tight, the bird is squeezed to death. If you're afraid of hurting the bird with a tight grip, you may hold your hands flat. Now when the bird flutters around, it falls to the

[28] This is a male perspective of shoe shopping. I'm sure that, for some females, the process of selecting shoes is a much deeper and more involved process.

[29] I've had some personal experience in holding baby birds, so when Henri Nouwen makes this connection in *Lifesigns* (New York: Doubleday, 1986, p. 34), it makes a whole lot of sense to me.

ground where it may be wounded and isn't protected from predators. The best way to hold this tiny bird is to cup your hands, to create an open space where the bird can flap its wings, to create a free space that has structure and security so the bird can't seriously hurt itself.

You can help students learn how to reflect by creating cupped-hand opportunities for students to wrestle with the way experiences might impact their lives.

If the learning loop were to stop at the reflection stage, it would still be missing a vital piece. When we reflect, we gain important new perspectives about the information and about ourselves. We don't want to be like the man who looks in the mirror only to walk away and forget what he sees.[30] Reflection that doesn't impact how we live, think, and believe is just as hollow as an idea that is never lived.

Re-view

Reflection gives us perspective on what has happened when we have applied new information. This new perspective leads us to the next step in the learning loop: re-view. To re-view is to take another look at the information presented, using the perspective given to us by reflection. This perspective allows us to see the information in a different light.

Re-view involves the hard work of critical thinking, evaluation, and assessment. It's the time to reformulate the original information into a plan that better fits the individual. This new information grows from the practical application and reflection that the student experienced.

Honesty and integrity are vital to the quality of the re-view. Failures need to be claimed just as enthusiastically as successes. The new information provided by trying out an application is just as important as how effective the application was. Every experience becomes an opportunity to learn, grow, and progress. As we look at any experience with perspective gained by reflection and the desire to learn, we discover the amazing reality that God has packed our lives with opportunities to grow closer to him and love the people around us.

You may have noticed where the re-view step has left us. We now have new information that can be applied. This is the loopiness of the learning loop. We enter into the same steps as before on the same topic but with new information and from a new height. One loop will help us see the information differently. Allowing the loop to continue begins a process that encourages ongoing transformation.

The Dynamics

Beside understanding the components of the Amazing Learning Loop of Depth, we also need to understand how the loop works—the dynamics. Understanding the parts is the first step, but understanding how these parts interact helps you use this model intentionally. When you fully understand that the learning loop is sequential, cyclical, and intentional, it becomes practical and useful in your ministry.

The order of the learning loop is important and semi-static. This means that each step in the loop builds off the one before it and sets up the one after it. You

30 See James 1:23-25.

can enter into the loop at any step, but if you skip steps then you miss some of the power.

The great part of the learning loop is that it's loopy,[31] a continuous cycle.

Each loop creates increased levels of understanding and assures that new behaviors become part of our lives. It's important to have opportunities to try gained knowledge and to refine it by repetition. Linking several learning loops creates a spiral rather than a circle. Each time you go through a loop your experience happens at a different level. You continually improve and grow even though you may be going through the same types of things.

The Amazing Learning Loop of Depth can be intentionally used in designing programs and predicting the needs of an individual or group. If you can identify which step of the loop is happening, you can prepare for the next step. If you present some new information in a lesson you can also create an opportunity for the students to try it out. After going out on a service project, allow a few minutes for people to write or just be silent to reflect on the experience. This model gives you clues about where people are in the learning process and helps you choose what comes next wisely and intentionally.

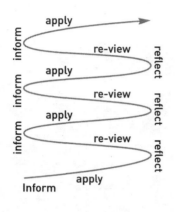

Figure 1-6
**Amazing Learning
Loop of Depth - side view**

Program Navigation

Here's an exercise you can try using The Amazing Learning Loop of Depth—Program Navigation. When you use a compass you need to know where you've come from and where you are if you want to chart a course for where you want to go. You'll need a journal or a few pieces of paper. Choose one aspect of your ministry to focus on (Sunday morning meeting, mid-week Bible study).

Think back on the past two months. Grab notes or schedules from these meeting if you have them. Can you identify any parts of the learning loop? Have you linked any loops?

Next, focus on your last meeting. What part of the learning loop did you end on? Did you leave them with new information? Was your last event an application, such as a service project?

Now you have a basic idea of where you've been and where you're at. What step should come next according to the learning loop? Now you can plot a course for the future.

Linking Loops

Another way you can use this model is to link two or three loops into one program. Start with new information or an activity and then follow the loop. Build in reflection opportunities and structured re-view times. After the event, set aside some time to make a map or a flow chart of what happened. Where did you start? What changed by the time you were finished? Were there any surprises? What would come next in the loop?

You'll find more about using The Amazing Learning Loop of Depth in Planning Exercises (page 110) and Appendix A (page 148).

[31] Loopy as in "like a loop," not as in "crazy"—and another opportunity to use a fun word.

Experiential Methods and the Bible

You are walking down a country road. It is a quiet afternoon. You look up and far, far down the road you see someone walking toward you. You are surprised to have noticed someone so far away. But you keep walking, expecting nothing more then a friendly nod as you pass. He gets closer. You see he has bright orange hair. He is closer—a white satin suit spotted with colored dots. Closer—a painted white face and red lips. You and he are fifty yards apart. You and a full-fledged clown holding a bicycle horn are twenty yards apart. You approach on the lonely country road. You nod. He honks and passes.

—STEVE MARTIN IN CRUEL SHOES, (PUTNAM, 1979)

When was the last time you unexpectedly passed by a clown on a lonely country road? My guess is it's been a while. This is an odd, outrageous experience. But encountering the clown is not what makes this story worth reading. What makes this passage interesting is that the observer makes no comment. The reader's curiosity is piqued by an outrageous moment, yet the clown and the passerby both miss the moment.

Come on! It's a clown! You have to say something. At least "Hi. Nice horn." Or "Who does your hair? I can never find that shade of orange."[32] Even if you had some sort of traumatic clown experience as a child, you would have some sort of reaction. The experience is just too unique not to have some sort of impact.

Now, let's think about a different situation. You see a man walking down the street. One person stands out from the crowd. Something is noticeably different about him. He seems to be wearing a yoke, a big wooden collar that would, in normal circumstances, be worn by a cow or an ox. As he gets closer, there is no doubt that this man is walking the streets wearing a yoke.

Many questions swirl in your brain, mainly "Why is this guy wearing a yoke?"

[32] I'm assuming that orange is not his natural color, but I think I'm safe with that assumption.

You don't wake up in the morning and accidentally grab a farming implement out of your closet instead of a coat.[33] No, this isn't a mistake. He's done this on purpose, and he can't wait to tell you why.

By wearing a yoke, this man, Jeremiah, found a powerful way to get his message across, a message crucial to the survival of whole nations. Mere words were not enough. God instructed Jeremiah not only to deliver the message but also to create an experience that would impact his audience deeply and powerfully.

Through Jeremiah, God chose to use experience to get his message across. In fact, God often used experiential methods to get his messages across.

In ministry we spend a lot of time considering the meaning of Scripture but not much time looking at the methods used in Scripture to teach. The Bible is filled with examples of teachers and leaders who tapped into the experiences of people to help them grow and lead them closer to God. In this chapter let's focus on the methodology in Scripture rather than theology—how God teaches rather than what he teaches.

Parables

Parables are a powerful way to use common, everyday events to teach insightful, uncommon lessons. What's the difference between a parable and a story? Not much really. A parable is a story with a few specific characteristics. While the purpose of some stories is just to be entertaining, parables teach something as well. Parables tend to be short and ask the listeners to call on some common experiences. Jesus often used this method in his teaching, but we find parables throughout the Bible.

Let's pull apart a couple parables to see how they work. This parable from Jesus is a good place to start:

The kingdom of heaven is like treasure hidden in a field. When a man found it, he hid it again, and then in his joy went and sold all he had and bought that field.
—Matthew 13:44

Who of us hasn't dreamed of finding a hidden treasure? This story can be so short—two sentences—because Jesus referred to a powerful experience we all share. At the mention of treasure our brains may picture old wooden chests overflowing with gold or jewels.[34] This universal hope for treasure not only moves the story along quickly but also makes it powerful. Because it's so familiar, it's close to our hearts. We know this part of the story so well that we're willing to let down our guard and open ourselves up to the rest of the story.

The rest of the story is a surprise. Let's say you find a car for sale with a big stash of cash in the glove box. We would expect Jesus to tell us to be honest and tell the owner about this stash of cash. But no! Jesus says to keep it hidden, scrounge up all the cash you can, and pay the seller.[35] Finding a way to keep the cash is something we would all think about, but not something we would share with anyone. We're given the opportunity to be ourselves. This twist is what gets us talking.

Three elements in this story make it an experiential parable.

[33] I have accidentally grabbed mismatching socks and often find myself wearing clothes that clash mightily, but even I couldn't make this kind of fashion blunder.

[34] For me it looks a lot like the pirate's booty in the Pirates of the Caribbean ride at Disneyland. How a pirate's treasure would be in a field in first-century Palestine, I'm not sure.

[35] This puts a new spin on WWJD.

First, it calls on an experience common to all who are listening. It focuses on the experience of the listener not the experience of the teacher. There is no need to embellish the telling of the story because everyone already knows the context. This is an important difference between parables and other stories. The experience has already happened in the life of the learner.

Common experience allows for the second element of a parable: the opportunity to reveal ourselves. The story has entered a part of our lives that is well known, so we feel safe to respond naturally. When we feel safe, we're more likely to allow our real thoughts and feelings to surface. We respond without thinking, without trying to impress anyone. We're allowed to be who we really are. This kind of involvement creates the potential for the story to circumvent our personal defenses.

Once we're sucked into the story by a familiar experience and feel free to be ourselves, we're open to the twist in the conclusion, which allows us to see the old experience in a new way. And that's where we find the teaching. The parable gets around any defenses we've built up to guard our hearts so the lesson can touch us deeply.

Let's take a look at a parable from the Old Testament to see if we can learn more about how parables work.

King David is having an affair with Bathsheba. God gives Nathan the unenviable job of pointing out the flaws of the most powerful man in the kingdom to the most powerful man in the kingdom. Nathan uses a parable that calls on experiences from David's childhood: caring for sheep.

The Lord sent Nathan to David. When he came to him, he said, "There were two men in a certain town, one rich and the other poor. The rich man had a very large number of sheep and cattle, but the poor man had nothing except one little ewe lamb he had bought. He raised it, and it grew up with him and his children. It shared his food, drank from his cup and even slept in his arms. It was like a daughter to him.

"Now a traveler came to the rich man, but the rich man refrained from taking one of his own sheep or cattle to prepare a meal for the traveler who had come to him. Instead, he took the ewe lamb that belonged to the poor man and prepared it for the one who had come to him."

David burned with anger against the man and said to Nathan, "As surely as the Lord lives, the man who did this deserves to die! He must pay for that lamb four times over, because he did such a thing and had no pity."

Then Nathan said to David, "You are the man." —2 Samuel 12:1-7

He knew he couldn't just go to David and tell him he was in sin and needed to stop. David's defenses were up. Nathan could have found himself missing some important part of his body. Instead he used an experience from David's life to open up an opportunity for David to hear this important lesson.

David's childhood was spent with sheep, and he knew how the poor man could feel so close to his lamb. He had first-hand experience in holding lambs close to his chest. David knew what it took to care for and protect lambs. He not only thought that this lamb was the poor man's joy, he felt that same love. This story put David back into his wonder years, caring for his father's flocks. When Nathan chose to talk about sheep, he knew David would be intrigued. This story goes straight to his heart, so when Nathan throws in the twist, David reveals his true feelings.

When Nathan reveals the deeds of the rich man, David explodes with anger. He has lost himself in his own childhood experience and allows his true self to come to the surface. David the Shepherd speaks to David the King. The shepherd felt the pain and loss of the poor man; the king had the power to do something about it. The compassionate anger of the shepherd meets the justice of the king. The story frees David to respond, true to his past role as shepherd and current role as king.

At this point David's defenses are flattened. He's open to the hard lesson Nathan delivers. The information that could have resulted in Nathan's execution goes straight to David's soul and reveals the magnitude of his sin.[36] His resistance disappears, and the lesson transforms David from a killer and an adulterer into a man desperate for forgiveness.

These two stories show how parables tap into experience to reveal powerful lessons. They work by using the preexisting experiences of the audience, which creates a safe place for learners to respond as their real selves. Their defenses are relaxed, and they're able to hear the lessons, be impacted by them deeply, and be transformed.

Object lessons

An object lesson takes an ordinary item from everyday life and attaches meaning to it. A stick is no longer a piece of wood but a symbol for a nation. Flowers, when used in an object lesson, represent God's concern for our everyday needs. Now whenever you pick up a stick or see a flower you think of the lessons connected to them.

Let's take a look at two object lessons in the Bible to see how they work.

"And why do you worry about clothes? See how the lilies of the field grow. They do not labor or spin. Yet I tell you that not even Solomon in all his splendor was dressed like one of these. If that is how God clothes the grass of the field, which is here today and tomorrow is thrown into the fire, will he not much more clothe you, O you of little faith?"

—Matthew 6:28-30

Jesus offers this object lesson near the end of the Sermon on the Mount. The crowds were gathering around him, so he went up on a hill and asked his closest followers to sit and listen. Being outside and up on a hill, they must have had a great view of the surrounding valley.[37]

When Jesus says, "See how the lilies of the field grow," he's taking an ordinary object, a lily, from their lives and focusing their attention on it. His listeners lived in a rural society where they walked through fields every day. They would notice the lilies like we might notice flowers in a flowerpot. Occasionally we might pass by and comment on their beauty or enjoy the scent, but rarely do we give them a second thought. Jesus selects the everyday occurrence of passing through a field and holds it out to be looked at in a new way. The first step in an object lesson is to choose a

[36] Read Psalm 51 for David's response.

[37] They may have even been sitting in the middle of a field full of lilies.

familiar object to which meaning can be attached.

Next Jesus highlights specific characteristics or truths that are associated with the object, in this case, three aspects of the lilies: their lack of activity, their beauty, and their transience. The listeners wouldn't have to think twice about agreeing with these statements. Even if someone had never seen a lily before that moment, when Jesus points to the fields, that person would immediately recognize the accuracy of the statements.

Many other statement could be made about the lilies, but Jesus selected these facts purposely. The purpose is not to understand everything about lilies. The object of an object lesson is never the true focus. The object gives us something tangible, something solid to experience, so it's easier for us to grasp complicated or difficult concepts. The truths about lilies lead to truths about life.

Jesus created an experience around a flower that will never let us look at flowers the same way again. He has connected God's concern for our everyday need for clothing to the experience of looking at flowers. It's a lesson presented once, but one that continues to teach every time we pass by a field or a flower arrangement. The power of an object lesson is that learners gain new understanding right away and continue to remember the lesson with each experience of that object.

Notice one last thing about this object lesson: it starts before Jesus presents the object to be considered. The first phrase, "And why do you worry about clothes?" sets up the listeners' expectations. When Jesus starts talking about lilies, they know he's not planning to talk about farming or botany. He uses this preview as a hook, a way to draw the crowd into the lesson.

Look at this object lesson from one of the prophets to learn more.

"Son of man, take a stick of wood and write on it, 'Belonging to Judah and the Israelites associated with him.' Then take another stick of wood, and write on it, 'Ephraim's stick, belonging to Joseph and all the house of Israel associated with him.' Join them together into one stick so that they will become one in your hand.

"When your countrymen ask you, 'Won't you tell us what you mean by this?' say to them, 'This is what the Sovereign Lord says: I am going to take the stick of Joseph—which is in Ephraim's hand—and of the Israelite tribes associated with him, and join it to Judah's stick, making them a single stick of wood, and they will become one in my hand.' —Ezekiel 37:16-19

Tying two sticks together becomes more than construction or model making. God uses this simple task as an object lesson for the reunification of his people.

A stick is a simple prop. Sticks are singled out for an important lesson because joining sticks together wasn't anything new. It was a common task people were familiar with. What baits people is the writing on the sticks. That's different. There's something to learn because the teacher writes important names on each stick and ties them together. Unlike the man who encounters the clown in Steve Martin's story, people have to ask, "Why did he do that? What does it mean?"

This episode has all the classic features of an object lesson. The sticks are the object, and tying them together reveals the specific truths the teacher wants to high-light. The greater truth is God's desire to reunite the nation of Israel. The curiosity generated by writing on the sticks is what draws people into the lesson. Attaching meaning to objects is a simple way to help people grasp difficult ideas and creates continued learning every time people encounter the object.

Initiatives

You and your team stand at the edge of a wide river flowing with acid. Anything that touches this river instantly burns to a crisp. Your team has important skills and resources that must reach the other side. Your entire team must cross the acid river safely. You notice rocks that rise above the surface of the river, but they're too far apart to jump to. Your only resources are three 8-foot poles. The lives of millions depend on your success. Good luck.[38]

Not many real rivers in the world flow with acid. This river is defined by two ropes on a grassy field that make up an imaginary riverbank, and the rocks in the river are cinder bricks.

The team is participating in an activity specifically designed to give them an experience in problem-solving. While they may not be at a real acid river, they are interacting, communicating, conflicting, and solving the problem.

In experiential programming lingo, this is called an *initiative*—an activity or challenge that intentionally creates opportunities for people to learn and grow. An initiative can be as fanciful as this acid river challenge, or it can take place in a real-life setting. The steps taken to make this an intentional learning opportunity are what set initiatives apart from other experiences.

You can find this style of experiential teaching in many places in the Bible. Here are two examples.

After this the Lord appointed seventy-two others and sent them two by two ahead of him to every town and place where he was about to go. He told them, "The harvest is plentiful, but the workers are few. Ask the Lord of the harvest, therefore, to send out workers into his harvest field. Go! I am sending you out like lambs among wolves. Do not take a purse or bag or sandals; and do not greet anyone on the road.

"When you enter a house, first say, 'Peace to this house.' If a man of peace is there, your peace will rest on him; if not, it will return to you. Stay in that house, eat-ing and drinking whatever they give you, for the worker deserves his wages. Do not move around from house to house.

"When you enter a town and are welcomed, eat what is set before you. Heal the sick who are there and tell them, 'The kingdom of God is near you.' But when you enter a town and are not welcomed, go into its streets and say, 'Even the dust of your town that sticks to our feet we wipe off against you. Yet be sure of this: The kingdom of God is near.' I tell you, it will be more bearable on that day for Sodom than for that town.

—Luke 10:1-12

[38] See Acid River on page 63.

Crowds of people are following Jesus as he begins a journey to Jerusalem. He selects 72 for a special assignment—a challenge. It almost sounds like the introduction to Acid River.

"Okay, everybody find a partner. Have I got a challenge for you! Everybody paired up? Good. Here's the situation. There's a huge crop to bring in, but we don't have enough workers. It's up to you! But be careful. There's danger waiting for you. Don't let the wild animals keep you from completing your task."

Jesus chooses to have them work out this challenge in a real-life situation. It has a functional purpose; he wants to send out advance teams to villages he might visit.

But Jesus also sets specific guidelines about how this is to be accomplished. "Don't take any baggage. Don't greet anyone on the road. Stay in the same house while you're in a town." These limitations increase the difficulty of the task. Jesus uses these rules intentionally to set up the experience for learning. Not only will these disciples accomplish the task of scouting out villages, but they'll also walk away with a greater appreciation for God's power and faithfulness.

This isn't an intellectual exercise. It's not a theological discussion. Jesus doesn't say, "What if I were to send you out?" He sends them out. It's a real-life experience that demands action from the people who are learning. They have the opportunity to live the challenge and see the results.

When the disciples return they talk about what happened.[39] This debriefing time helps them understand what they learned. The function was complete, but the learning was solidified. Jesus took the time to help them understand the power and significance of their time on the road. Before they move on to the next experience, they take time to figure out what they've learned from this one. The lessons now change how they'll live in the future.

The activities in Luke 10 contain all the elements of a classic initiative: a specific challenge, rules that set up the experience for learning, taking on the task, and debriefing the experience.

In the Old Testament, we find this challenge in the midst of a series of challenge that God sets out for Gideon.

That same night the Lord said to him, "Take the second bull from your father's herd, the one seven years old. Tear down your father's altar to Baal and cut down the Asherah pole beside it. Then build a proper kind of altar to the Lord your God on the top of this height. Using the wood of the Asherah pole that you cut down, offer the second bull as a burnt offering." —Judges 6:25-26

Most of us remember Gideon as the guy with the fleece or as the guy whose army was too big.[40] But when we first meet him, he's hiding in a winepress.[41] The angel of the Lord greets this fearful man as "Mighty Warrior,"[42] and prepares him to live up to that name.

Tearing down the temple to Baal is his first task on his way to becoming what God knows he can be. The Lord gives him a specific assignment: tear down his father's temple and construct an altar to God. To Gideon, this is a great challenge. He's already fearful, and his task will make his family and his community angry. If

[39] See Luke 10:17.

[40] See Judges 6:36-40; 7:1-8.

[41] See Judges 6:11-12.

[42] An example of sarcastic prophecy?

he completes this task, his likely reward is bodily harm.

God gives Gideon guidelines to follow. He needs a bull to sacrifice, and he must build the altar with the wood from the temple. This isn't an intellectual exercise. Gideon must actually do it. Gideon must deal with his fear and accomplish the task.[43]

This event doesn't end with a new altar and a sacrificed bull. The next day Gideon is confronted. His learning isn't complete until after his actions and fears are in the open. Gideon stands in front of the people he offended to understand the value of the risk he took.

In Gideon's experience, we see all the elements of an initiative: a specific task, guidelines by which he must accomplish this task, action, and debriefing after the task to mark the lessons learned.

We find God using experiential methods throughout the Bible. The parables, object lessons, and initiative we've considered here are just a few. You can find many more. God uses experience to teach us.

This chapter separates methodology from theology. The surprise is that methodology reveals theology. By using experiential methods, God reveals the value of a person and his or her life. The learner has the freedom to discover the lesson rather than being forced to comply. Through this approach, we're also encouraged to be doers of the Word.[44]

In the same way, our methodology reveals our theology. How we teach reveals what we think of people and how the material should impact their lives. Experiential methods expose eternal truths to individuals so they can discover how they are uniquely impacted by that truth. They are then encouraged to let that truth transform their lives.

[43] He doesn't really overcome his fear as much as finds a way around it by sneaking in at night with his buddies to do the dirty work. Regardless, he still acted in the midst of his fear.

[44] See James 1:22.

Section Two

Activities and Exercises

Activities & Exercises

I've found the activities in this section to be fun, powerful, and effective. Each creates an opportunity to take advantage of experiential methods. You can do these just for fun,[45] but you'll lose their power and miss opportunities to change lives Unless you're intentional about using them—when you use them, how you introduce them, where you offer them, and how you sequence them.

The activities are broken into four categories. The format for each section is different because the purpose and context for each are different. The first and largest group is initiatives, which tend to be physical and interactive. The next section is made up of activities and exercises for small groups. The third category, large group activities, works with groups of 30 or more. The last group of exercises are used for planning and creating programs. Many of these activities and exercises are referenced in the chapter on program templates.

You don't need to let the stated location of activities limit your use. You can creatively modify them all for any context. In fact, I encourage you to use your imagination as you work with these activities.

One word of caution: *Always be aware of safety*. It's tough to walk away from a great learning experience if you can't walk away. Physical safety isn't the only type of safety. You and your leaders also need to create and maintain a safe place emotionally and socially. If you want your students to talk about tough, risky issues, they need to know they'll be heard and taken seriously. Adults need to model appropriate interaction and compassion with each other as well with students.[46]

Being experiential, many of these activities are difficult to capture into words and confine to the pages of a book. This book will help you better understand how to facilitate groups, but there's no substitute for interactive training. I highly recommend participating in these activities through facilitator training workshops and seminars. Though many are focused on challenge courses or camps, the skills are easily transferred to a youth ministry context.[47] You'll gain practical insights that can't be written in any book.

As you read through these activities, you may recognize some of them. Maybe you know one by a different name or another as having different props. To be honest, there are few totally original activities listed in this section. What you will find

[45] I say "just" to mean "only for fun," not to diminish the importance of fun. I believe fun and joy are important parts of ministry and are valuable to explore.

[46] As you can tell from some of my footnotes, I enjoy sarcastic comments. However, sarcasm, though it may be fun and funny, often works against creating an emotionally and socially safe environment.

[47] This book will help you transfer skills and knowledge to youth ministry.

are activities I've used and find to work well in a youth ministry context. It's not a definitive collection of experiential activities either. It's a practical collection to help you get started.

Through the years, I've modified and adapted these activities to my particular style, but they all have their roots in others' ideas. The people who originated these ideas deserve credit, but the problem is finding the original source. Many of these activities can be found in multiple resources. Another complicating factor is that many experiential activities are passed along orally or as a part of other programs. Let me honor them:[48]

Karl Rohnke's books, *Cowstails and Cobras II*, *Silver Bullets*, and *The Bottomless Bag*, contain a huge number of quality activities and offer great insight into adventure programming.

Jim Cain and Barry Jolliff offer a wonderful collection of activities and insights in *Teamwork & Teamplay*. I've also learned a lot by talking and playing with Jim at several conferences. He offers great training, workshops, and resources through his organization, Teamwork & Teamplay.

Tom Leahy at Leahy & Associates is another great source of information and inspiration for me. Each year Tom hosts an amazing conference[49] for people who lead experiential activities.

Chris Cavert continually compiles activities. His collections of games for teachers (and other books) are great resources. Through my contact with him at conferences over the years, Chris has contributed immensely to my bag of tricks.

Playing and learning with Dave Vermilye, Dick Hammond, and Lisa Blockus has definitely influence what you find in this section.

Some of the more interpersonal and emotion-based activities come directly from my association with Joe Slevcove and Sheri Bunn, two actors who introduced me to the power of drama exercises.

The Disclaimer

I've done my best to offer powerful activities that increase your effectiveness as a pastor, leader, and teacher, and to explain them so you can use them safely, but there are limits to how effectively I can do this in a book. There are risks to using this material.

Experiential activities can present elements of physical, emotional, and interpersonal risk. This book is a reference source only. I cannot assume liability or responsibility for how anyone uses or applies the information in this book.. This includes errors and accidents due to omission of details, misprints, or typographical errors. You assume the ultimate responsibility for judging the suitability and safety of each activity for your situation.

The intent of this material is to introduce the idea of experiential methods in the context of youth ministry. Neither this book nor any other book can replace practical experience, training, and education. I strongly encouraged you to seek professional training before you begin using the activities.

Enjoy and be safe!

[48] For details about some of the available resources, see Appendix C, page 152.

[49] NCCPS—The National Challenge Course Practitioners Symposium. Quite a mouthful to say, but probably the best conference I attend.

Initiative Activities

Chapter 2.1

The activities found in this section create controlled experiences that you can use to teach specific lessons or to allow groups to explore their relationships. They can be fun, active, and intense. While each one can be used independently, they can also be used sequentially to increase the power and effectiveness of the experiences. Most of these activities can be done inside or outside with simple props or no props at all, but some, as I've noted, should be done only outside or only as part of a professionally built and facilitated low-challenge course.

Each activity is presented in a format intended to help you use it effectively.

- **Activity Brief**—The explanation of how to present and lead the activity.

- **Equipment**—A list of supplies you need.

- **Safety**—Specific safety issues to watch for. Since every situation presents unique hazards and concerns, use your own best judgment.

- **Consider This**—Since the activities are intended to be learning experiences, a list of things to watch for, questions to ask, issues to address—a starting point— is also included. You'll find these activities present many rich topics for discussion that aren't included in this list.

- **Variations**—Options for increasing the difficulty, adding interest, or otherwise increasing the impact of the activity.

- **Personal Notes and Re-View**—Each time you lead an activity, take time to make notes about what worked, what didn't work, interesting behaviors or interactions, possible variations, ways to preview the activity. Here's your space to reflect and re-view to make the activity your own.

You'll notice that some activities have creative names that may be associated with a fun story used to introduce the activity.[50] I've chosen not to develop these stories so that you'll invent your own. Creating appropriate scenarios, allegories, and imagery can greatly increase the power of these activities. In your planning, create fun stories to explain the challenge and engage imaginations.

SPOTTING AND CALL-RESPONSE SEQUENCE

ACTIVITY BRIEF
Before a group does any activity that involves lifting or carrying people they should learn to spot and to use the call-response sequence[51]—and practice them. This activity builds trust and teaches the call-response command sequence used in other activities.

1. Gather the group around you.
2. Model a good *ready position*. Feet should be about shoulder width apart with one foot slightly in front of the other. Knees should be slightly bent, and the back should be straight. Arms should be extended to the front, elbows bent and at about chest height. Their hands should be open and palms toward the person being spotted.
3. Have the group practice the ready position. Participants should feel comfortable and stable. Check individual positions.
4. Have the group break into pairs.
5. Teach them the call-response sequence.

Faller: "Spotter ready?"
Spotter: "Ready!"
Faller: "Falling?"[52]
Spotter: "Fall on!"

Have the group members practice the call-response sequence; then have the faller lean into the spotter so that she has to support the faller's weight.

It's important to remember that spotting does not mean catching the faller's whole body. The spotter makes sure that, in a real fall, the faller's feet hit the ground first.

EQUIPMENT
None

SAFETY
This is all about safety. Have participants start off with easy leaning and progress toward supporting more of the faller's weight.

CONSIDER THIS
Make sure everyone gives the call-response sequence properly. This is an opportu-

[50] Spider's Web, Acid River, and Plane Crash are initiatives that use stories for the setup.

[51] This call-response sequence is similar to what's used in trust falls, high-challenge course elements, and rock climbing.

[52] Notice that this is a question. After asking, "Falling?" the person waits for the spotters to respond before he actually begins to fall.

nity to assess how much the group is able to handle.

PERSONAL NOTES AND RE-VIEW

SILLY STRETCHES

ACTIVITY BRIEF

Warming up is an important part of any activity-based program. Silly Stretches warms up bodies—and attitudes too.

1. Have the group form a circle.[53]
2. Remind them about the importance of warming up their bodies and their attitudes.
3. Begin with traditional stretches such as touching their toes and twisting at the waist.
4. Increase the challenge with see-if-you-can stretches. "See if you can touch your nose to your knee. See if you can touch your shoulder blades together."
5. As the group gets warmed up, make the stretches funnier and more ridiculous.

_ Freestyle ski jumps—"Can you do a daffy? A spread eagle? A helicopter?"
_ The Couch Potato—"Pretend you're sitting on a couch. Reach for those chips. Reach for that remote."
_ Swimming—"Lie on the ground and swim freestyle. Now the breaststroke."

EQUIPMENT
_ An open surface
_ A list of stretches

SAFETY

Remember that this is a real-life warm-up time. Start slow and easy. Don't ask the group to do anything too strenuous or risky at first. Build up to more difficult stretches.

CONSIDER THIS

Stretches are great for early in the program. This is also an opportunity to observe who's willing to take risks physically or socially. You may get an idea of what roles individuals will play in the group interactions.

[53] If you're really daring and countercultural, you can have them stand in a line.

VARIATIONS

Be imaginative as you develop stretches.

PERSONAL NOTES AND RE-VIEW

WEIGHT SHARE

ACTIVITY BRIEF

Before the group attempts any lifting exercises, ease them into the process by doing this activity.

1. Have the group break into pairs. Partners should be approximately the same height and weight.
2. Explain that they'll be increasing their trust in their partners through the amount of weight they place on them.
3. Have them lean into their partners hand to hand.
4. Allow them to then create ways to place more and more weight until they have transferred all of their weight to their partners.

EQUIPMENT

None

SAFETY

This is the time to practice taking responsibility for each other and to build trust. It's a low-level trust activity, but it lays a foundation for increased trust in the future.

CONSIDER THIS

How creative do the pairs get about weight sharing? How are the pairs challenged by this activity? Is a factor in developing trust how well they know their partners?

VARIATIONS

Try sharing weight among three or more people.

PERSONAL NOTES AND RE-VIEW

BLIND THWACKER

ACTIVITY BRIEF

In a scene from *Star Wars*, Luke Skywalker deflects laser blasts from a floating robot with his light saber while blindfolded. This activity is like that—except there's no floating robot or light saber, and we're not in space. It does involve a blindfold however. This is a fun challenge that allows people to choose their own level of involvement.

1. One member of the group is blindfolded and given a thwacker.[54] This person is the designated thwacker—the DT.
2. The group stands in a fairly large circle[55] around the DT.
3. The DT, while blindfolded, tries to keep the others from touching her by brandishing the thwacker.
4. The group's challenge is for someone to sneak in and touch the DT without getting hit with the thwacker.
5. Whoever manages to touch the DT becomes the next blindfolded, thwacker-swinging DT.

EQUIPMENT

_ 1 thwacker per group
_ 1 blindfold
_ Open space—This is a great outdoor activity but can be done indoors if the room is large enough and the ceiling is high enough.

[54] A thwacker is a 4- to 8-foot length of pipe insulation tubing, also known as a boffer or a noodle.

[55] *Fairly large* is a relative term. The group should start at least five yards away from the DT.

SAFETY

You need to be especially concerned about safety whenever anyone is blindfolded or swinging an object. This activity has both. Make sure you choose a location that's free of potential hazards[56] that might be a problem for someone who's blindfolded. The thwacker is soft, so it's not particularly dangerous to swing around. When the thwacker hits someone, it produces a satisfying pop but no pain.

CONSIDER THIS

This activity can be used to energize a group after lunch or during a break. During a debrief, you might explore what it's like to loose your vision and how to use other senses to compensate. Most of the time people approach this challenge as individuals. Did the group ever try a cooperative approach? What were individual strategies?

VARIATIONS

Put two DTs in the middle. Or to increase the challenge for the entire group, require the DT to call out "blind" and the rest of the group to respond by yelling "thwacker."[57]

PERSONAL NOTES AND RE-VIEW

[56] Such as sprinkler heads, gopher holes, sharp pointy sticks, and cars traveling at high speeds.

[57] You don't have to use *blind thwacker. Marco Polo, peanut butter* or *adjective-noun* work just as well.

[58] This is one of the few activities whose roots are certain. Tom Smith wrote *Raccoon Circle*, a book that offers tons of activities that use loops of webbing. Tom and Jim Cain wrote a follow-up to that book, *The Book on Racoon Circles* (see Resources on page 152), with even more ideas.

[59] For you non-knot people, a hitch is a simple knot. You know it if you've ever tied rubber bands together.

WEBBING CIRCLES

ACTIVITY BRIEF

This is a series of challenges using six- to 10-foot loops of tubular webbing.[58]

1. Have the group stand in a circle holding hands.
2. Start by breaking the circle in one spot and have those two people reach through the loop of webbing before holding hands.
3. The goal is for the group to move the loop of webbing completely around the circle until it reaches the place where it started without separating hands.
4. After the group has completed this, add another loop, perhaps at another point in the circle. Have the group move the loops in opposite directions.
5. The last stage of this challenge is to attach the two loops with a simple hitch[59] and have the loops move in opposite directions.

EQUIPMENT

_ Two loops of webbing per group

SAFETY

Make sure people don't hold on too tightly to each other's hands. The risk of webbing burns or restricted blood flow is low, but watch for it anyway.

CONSIDER THIS

This simple activity can create rich interactions. How do they respond to each new step in the challenge? Do they help each other? How are they helping each other? How do they act—and feel—when they aren't near the loop? Who had both loops at the same time? How did the participant deal with that?

VARIATIONS

After the group has done these challenges, go back to one loop. Challenge them to see how fast they can get everyone through the loop. Push them to improve each time. Challenge them to think of different ways to accomplish the task.

PERSONAL NOTES AND RE-VIEW

TEAM ON A T-SHIRT

ACTIVITY BRIEF

If you don't have a T-Shirt, you can use a bandanna, loop of rope, or similar item. The key is in how you explain the task.

1. Lay the T-shirt on the ground. If you're using a loop of rope, be generous with the amount of space to start.
2. Ask the group to agree on a simple song that everyone knows.[60]
3. Challenge the group by saying, "Everyone in the group must have one foot on the T-shirt and one foot in the air."[61] They must stay there for as long as it takes them to sing the song. While you are saying this, stand on the T-shirt and lift one foot off the ground. That's one way to interpret the rules—but the rules say nothing about having to stand.
4. Make the space smaller after each success.

[60] "Twinkle, Twinkle, Little Star," or maybe their favorite praise song.

[61] Using these words is important.

EQUIPMENT

_ A large T-shirt, rope, bandanna, or a similar item to define the small area

SAFETY

There's a risk of the group falling over, so be aware of the playing surface. Walk around and give assistance if the group starts to tip over. Don't allow the group to stack up or lift anyone off the ground.[62]

CONSIDER THIS

Does the group listen to what you say the rules are, or do they simply model your behavior? Groups often use the strategy you model until that model no longer works—a great example of the power of modeling.

Listen for the first suggestion of another way to think about this challenge. Sometimes the first suggestion is ignored or seen as cheating.

Is the group exploring other resources? Time—do they sing faster? Personnel—do they arrange themselves by strength, weight, balancing skills? Space—do they arrange their feet? Stand on toes?

VARIATIONS

Elevator Up is a simple variation that completely changes this activity. Instead of "one foot on the T-shirt (or circle) and one foot in the air," tell them that the T-shirt (or circle) is an elevator and is the only thing that can hold weight. Nothing can touch outside the area until they finish singing.

PERSONAL NOTES AND RE-VIEW

WIND IN THE WILLOWS OR WILLOWS IN THE WIND

ACTIVITY BRIEF

Whether as a part of a trust sequence or as a way to get ready for other lifting activities, Wind in the Willows is a fun and safe way to practice mutual support and physical trust.

1. Teach the group how to spot and give the call-response sequence (see Spotting and Call-Response Sequence on page 40).
2. One member—the faller—stands in the middle with arms crossed and folded against her chest. She stands straight and keeps her feet in one spot.
3. When the faller is ready, she begins the call-response sequence.

4. The group catches her and *gently* passes her around and across the circle until she's finished.

5. Then the group members gently stands her up. Make sure the group continues to support her until she says she is balanced.

6. Invite everyone to take a turn.

EQUIPMENT

_ Open space

_ A safe landing surface

SAFETY

As long as the group takes this activity seriously, it's safe. Make sure they use the call-response sequence so everyone really is ready when the faller falls.

Stress the idea of *gently* passing the person. Don't let the team push or shove the faller.

CONSIDER THIS

Trust and responsibility are two issues that often arise from this activity. Look for signs of nervousness or anxiety as you invite people to be in the middle. Ask the group how the call-response sequence might impact the faller's anxiety level. A mixed or mumbled "We're ready" may not inspire confidence, but a loud, enthusiastic response may help people overcome their fear.

VARIATIONS

Instead of standing in a circle, have the people in the circle on their knees. They support the middle person by touching only the knees and thighs.

PERSONAL NOTES AND RE-VIEW

FALLING AND CATCHING

ACTIVITY BRIEF

This activity offers a high level of perceived risk, but it's actually safe if done properly.[63]

1. Teach the group to spot and to use the call-response sequence.[64]

2. Have everyone line up in front of the platform in two lines. They should be standing face to face about two feet apart. Everyone places their hands in front of them,

[63] Notice this is not called a trust fall. This activity can be about so much more than trust.

[64] See Spotting and Call-Response Sequence on page 40.

palms up. Their hands should be interlaced like a zipper. Do not have them hold each other's hands.

3. Once the lines are arranged, invite one member of the group to stand on the platform with you.

4. Position the faller with his back to the group, arms crossed and folded against his chest.

5. Instruct the faller to stay stiff and not to bend at the waist as he falls.

6. The facilitator also needs to make sure the group is properly lined up to make the catch before the faller starts the command sequence. The group should only respond "We're ready!" when everyone is in the ready position.

7. The person falls back and is caught by the group.

8. Invite everyone in the group to give it a try.

EQUIPMENT

_ A rock, platform, or table no more then five feet high.[65] Make sure it's stable and designed to support two people standing on it.

SAFETY

Make sure the group is mature enough to handle this activity. Build up to this activity with a series of lower risk exercises like Spotting and Call-Response Sequence (page 40), Weight Share (page 42), and Wind in the Willows (page 46).

Have fallers cross their arms and fold them into their chests to avoid injuring the catchers.[66]

Do not have the catchers hold hands.[67]

CONSIDER THIS

Trust is the major theme for this activity. Ask the group members what they can do to help build and diminish trust. Ask the fallers to describe the experience.

Explore the issue of responsibility. What's it like to be a catcher?

Be sure to invite everyone to have a turn as the faller but never force anyone. Be sure the group doesn't use peer pressure to force anyone either.

VARIATIONS

Instead of falling backward, the person faces forward and jumps into the arms of the group members. Make sure that the group takes a step or two away from the platform and that the leaper jumps out and up at a 45-degree angle rather than diving down.

PERSONAL NOTES AND RE-VIEW

[65] A good rule for height is to never have the platform higher than the average eye level of the group.

[66] Almost all the injuries I've seen have been to the catchers as a result of fallers' flailing arms.

[67] Catchers bonking heads because they were holding hands is the only other injury I've witnessed besides the arm flailing.

NAME TOSS

ACTIVITY BRIEF

If the participants are new to each other—or if a few new people have joined the group—Name Toss is an easy way to learn names because they're repeated many times.

1. Have the group stand in a circle.
2. Explain the purpose of the activity is to help them learn and remember group members' names.
3. Produce the tossable object.[68]
4. People can toss to whomever they want, but encourage them to toss the object to people they don't know.
5. The person tossing the object says her own name first, then the name of the person the object is tossed to. People may ask names before throwing.
6. Model this by first asking a group member's name, saying your own name followed by the other person's name, and tossing the object.
8. The person who catches the object repeats the process by saying his name and someone else's name and tossing the object.
9. Allow them to continue the process until people have said their names at least once (if the group is large) or several times (if the group is small). Be sure to stop before they get bored.

EQUIPMENT

_ One tossable object (or more)—Choose odd or funny objects to toss to increase the laughter
_ Plenty of space

SAFETY

This activity is about tossing, not throwing. Even the softest plush toy can cause damage if it's thrown hard enough.

CONSIDER THIS

This is a fun way to break the ice and to help people start using names. How willing are people to ask names? Do they remember to use their own names first or do they only use the names they're tossing to?

VARIATIONS

Once one object has been tossed a few times, add another so the two objects are being tossed at the same time. Add as many as you like. Use this as a way to start Warp Speed (page 50) or Team Juggling (page 51).

PERSONAL NOTES AND RE-VIEW

[68] An object is tossable if it can fit in one hand, is soft, and doesn't have any pointy edges. Nerf balls—tossable. Baseballs—not. Stuffed animals—tossable. Knives—not. Chains—not.

WARP SPEED

ACTIVITY BRIEF

With just one tossable object, this activity creates opportunities for amazingly deep learning.

1. Have the group stand in a circle.
2. Give one person in the group a tossable object.[69]
3. Tell the group that they'll need to remember the pattern of throws the object moves in. Have them toss the object around the circle in a random pattern until everyone has touched it once. The same person starts and ends with the object.
4. Once they've created the pattern, the challenge is to see how fast they can complete that sequence correctly without dropping the object.

There are creative ways to accomplish this task, but all the group members can't touch the object at the same time.

EQUIPMENT
_ A tossable object
_ A timer, such as a stopwatch
_ Plenty of space

SAFETY
Remind everyone to toss, not throw, the object. Be sure you have enough space and a good landing surface in case anyone makes a diving catch.

CONSIDER THIS
This activity generates a positive environment for creativity and self-motivation. Does the group experience tension between those striving for more and those who like "good enough"? Listen for how new ideas are handled. Watch for signs of the group's changing levels of energy and enthusiasm.

VARIATIONS
This activity works well as a follow-up to Name Toss (page 49). Instead of making this a timed event, see how many objects the group can keep going in the same pattern.

PERSONAL NOTES AND RE-VIEW

[69] An object is tossable if it can fit in one hand, is soft, and doesn't have any pointy edges. Nerf balls—tossable. Baseballs—not. Stuffed animals—tossable. Knives—not. Chains—not.

TEAM JUGGLING

ACTIVITY BRIEF

This activity starts out like Warp Speed (page 50) but goes in a different direction.

1. Have the group stand in a circle.
2. Give a tossable[70] object to one of the group members.
3. Have the group create a pattern by tossing the object back and forth across the circle. The pattern must include everyone and begin and end with the same person.
4. Have the group members practice the pattern once or twice to be sure they know it.
5. Introduce another tossable object to a different starting person.
6. Let the group establish a different pattern with the second object.
7. Have them practice to be sure they know the pattern.
8. Now challenge the group to do both patterns at the same time without dropping either object. If they drop an object or mess up the pattern, they start over.
9. Once the group can successfully handle two objects at the same time, introduce a third object to a new starter. Repeat the process. Continue to add objects to see how many patterns they can keep going at one time.

EQUIPMENT

_ 5 or more tossable objects (you get the idea)
_ Plenty of space

SAFETY

Encourage people to keep their tosses gentle.

CONSIDER THIS

If you don't tell the group you're going to add objects, they may start this activity thinking it'll be easy. As you add objects, listen for someone to say something like, "Now this is getting interesting!" That tells you when people are starting to feel challenged or when they're moving outside their comfort zones. In follow-up discussions, ask if anyone has had similar experiences or feelings at work, home, or school.

VARIATIONS

Use this activity as a follow-up to Name Toss (page 49) and Warp Speed (page 50).

Use a bouncy ball[71] as one of the tossable objects. Make the pattern more interesting by requiring group members to bounce it before it reaches the next person.

PERSONAL NOTES AND RE-VIEW

[70] An object is tossable if it can fit in one hand, is soft, and doesn't have any pointy edges. Nerf balls—tossable. Baseballs—not. Stuffed animals—tossable. Knives—not. Chains—not.

[71] A playground ball, a Super Ball, and even Silly Putty all qualify as bouncy balls.

CARABINEER WALK

ACTIVITY BRIEF

A carabineer is an oblong metal ring with one spring-hinged side. It's used primarily in mountain climbing as a connector and to hold a freely running rope. Help people understand being linked together as a team through this tangible experience.

1. Have group members tie the webbing loosely around their waists and clip the carabineer to it.
2. Direct participants to stand in circle and clip their carabineers to the webbing of the person to the right. They should all be attached together in a circle.
3. Take them on a walking adventure. Include obstacles such as going up and down stairs, through a split-rail fence, under a table, and between trees that are close together. Have them jog across an open area.

EQUIPMENT

_ Carabineers, one for each person—If you don't have carabineers, use short pieces of webbing, rope, or string.
_ Three-foot lengths of webbing or rope, one for each person

SAFETY

Be aware of everyone in the group as you lead them on this adventure. People may be pulled and tugged if the group isn't moving together. This is okay to a point, but stop the group immediately if anyone falls down.

Make sure group members feel that they can call for a safety stop at any time.

CONSIDER THIS

What's it like to be up front and leading? What's it like to be in the back? Who feels it if someone goes in a different direction than the rest of the group?

VARIATIONS

To make the group even closer together, clip an extra carabineer between carabineers that are across the circle from each other.

PERSONAL NOTES AND RE-VIEW

BLIND SQUARE

ACTIVITY BRIEF

Reveal the group's true dynamics through this challenging activity.

1. In a large open space, ask the group to gather together. Have everyone put on blindfolds.
2. After the blindfolds are in place, explain the challenge.
3. Place a length of rope into their hands and ask them to form a perfect square—while blindfolded—using the full length of the rope.
4. They are finished only when everyone is touching the rope and agrees that it's a perfect square.

EQUIPMENT

_ Blindfolds, one per person
_ 1 or more pieces of rope at least 20 feet long—The length of rope[72] depends on the number of people in the group and how much space is available.

SAFETY

Any activity that limits sight demands that you keep a close watch on all the group members. Be sure to choose an open space that doesn't have dangerous features such as holes, sprinklers, furniture, or pointy sticks. If anyone begins to approach a potentially dangerous obstacle, place yourself between the group member and the obstacle and tell them how much room they have. If the person gets too close, guide them to a safer place.

CONSIDER THIS

This one activity includes several challenges including geometry, communication, and moving around with impaired sight. Watch to see if the group takes time to plan. Or do they jump right in? How are ideas and solutions presented? How do the group members act on them?

Look for the tension between perfectionists and the good-enoughs. Watch for tension between people concerned about the end product and those concerned about process.

And what do people who do not have a specific task do?

VARIATIONS

To increase the challenge, place the rope on the ground near them rather than handing it to them.

To make it even more difficult, place a number of lengths of rope in their midst, and tell them to make the square using the full length of *all* the ropes. Don't tell them how many pieces of rope you've given them.

You have other options beside a square. The group can make any shape you choose, but the more sides and angles you require, the more difficult the task. Shapes with curves are extremely difficult.

You can add the issue of integrity into the mix by making blindfolds optional.

[72] The larger the rope, the more challenging this activity becomes.

Individuals can use the blindfolds if they don't think they can keep their eyes closed on their own.

For a subtle variation, use several kinds of line—webbing, string, climbing rope, and even bungee cord.

PERSONAL NOTES AND RE-VIEW

MAGIC CARPET

ACTIVITY BRIEF

Magic Carpet combines a fun problem-solving task with personal space encroachment.

1. Lay out the magic carpet, aka a tarp, blanket, or sheet.
2. Have the whole group stand on it.
3. The challenge is to turn over the magic carpet without anyone stepping off or touching the ground.

EQUIPMENT

_ A tarp, blanket or sheet, large enough for the whole group to stand on[73]
_ Open, level space

SAFETY

The space available becomes limited as this activity progresses. Piggybacking is allowed, but do *not* allow sitting on shoulders or stacking more than two high. Walk around to make sure no one gets into an unsafe position.

CONSIDER THIS

While each person starts with a bit of personal space, it's quickly reduced. Watch and listen to how the group responds to this diminishing space. Also listen to the problem-solving process. How are ideas presented and acted on?

[73] Make sure there isn't too much room. They should feel a bit crowded.

VARIATIONS

Start this activity off with a lot of room on the magic carpet. After the group turns over the carpet, fold it so that the area is smaller. Continue reducing the space as long as the group is engaged in the challenge.

PERSONAL NOTES AND RE-VIEW

COMPASS

ACTIVITY BRIEF

This activity is the blind leading the blind.

1. Blindfold everyone in the group.
2. Have the group choose a *worthy* destination for them to walk to blindfolded. Press the group to choose a goal that's challenging.

EQUIPMENT

_ Blindfolds, one for each person

SAFETY

You must look carefully for potential hazards as the group walks. Quietly let group members know if they are approaching a hazard.

CONSIDER THIS

Explore with the group what makes a goal worthy. How did they come to a decision on the destination? How did they communicate as they were walking? Ask the people walking in front to talk about their experience. Compare it to the perspective of the people walking in the back.

VARIATIONS

Add the issue of integrity to this activity by letting participants choose to wear blindfolds only if they think they can't keep their eyes closed.

Another way to increase the difficulty of this activity is to allow only one person to talk—or no one at all.

PERSONAL NOTES AND RE-VIEW

TEAM SKIS

ACTIVITY BRIEF
Walking on skis by yourself can be a big challenge. Try it with your whole team.

1. Place two team skis on the ground in front of the group. Ask everyone to stand with one foot on each ski.
2. Ask them pick up the ropes attached to the skis.
3. Using the ropes and lots of cooperation, they must remain on the skis and walk to and then around an object. They have to start over if anyone touches the ground.

EQUIPMENT
_ 2 team skis[74]
_ An object to maneuver around, such as a large rock, a tree, or an safety cone

SAFETY
Group members should be wearing closed-toe shoes.

To avoid injury, don't let participants wrap the ropes around their fingers, hands, or wrists.They should simply hold the ropes in their hands.

CONSIDER THIS
If even one person is out of sync, the group will go nowhere. Do group members take time to plan? How do they coordinate their steps?

Who leads? Is the leader the same one who coordinates the steps? Is the leader or coordinator near the front, the back, or the middle of the skis?

[74] Also known as trolleys. You can buy premade team skis or make them by drilling six holes in 2-inch by 6-inch boards that are ten feet long. Thread a rope through each hole and tie knots on both ends so that it can't slip through.

VARIATIONS

Have the group complete an obstacle course.

Add another ski so that half the group has a foot on the left ski, the other half of the group has a foot on the right ski, and they all have a foot on the middle ski.

PERSONAL NOTES AND RE-VIEW

LINE-UPS

ACTIVITY BRIEF

This is a fun, physical, problem-solving task that also helps break down barriers.

1. Ask the entire group to balance on a log.
2. Challenge them to rearrange so they're standing from shortest to tallest. They can't step off the log nor can they use any outside source, such as a tree branch, to keep balanced.

EQUIPMENT

_ A log—Really all you need is a long, narrow, defined area: a curb, bench, rope, or tape line on the ground.

SAFETY

Be available to spot tricky moves. Be aware of people who have larger-than-usual personal space or issues about being touched in some way.[75] Though they don't come up often, these issues change the dynamics of the challenge.

CONSIDER THIS

Does the group take time to plan? How do they move around each other? What's the best way to pass? Is the "best way" the best for everyone?

VARIATIONS

Your imagination can generate many ways of lining up. Try arranging by age, month

[75] These issues may arise because of circumstances as horrible as earlier abuse or as ordinary as commitment to a sport. I once facilitated a group with a dancer who was extremely sensitive about having her feet touched. If you keep pushing people like this to stay involved, you can push them into emotional crisis. Difficult issues like these can be addressed with additional facilitation training. In the meantime, don't unpack anything that you can't repack.

of birth, or hat size. Increase the challenge by having them rearrange by shoe size without talking.

PERSONAL NOTES AND RE-VIEW

EXPLOSIVES

ACTIVITY BRIEF

Have fun creating a story to encompass this activity. It's a great way to look at problem solving, trust, and imagination.

1. Select three members of the group to become *the bomb*.
2. When they join hands, the bomb is activated. The bomb will explode if any of their hands are separated or if the bomb is treated or handled roughly. Since bombs are inanimate objects, the three people who are part of the bomb can't help in any way.
3. The rest of the group must transport the bomb to a safe spot, some distance away, where it can be detonated safely. Once the bomb is lifted from the ground it can't be set down until it reaches the safe spot or it will explode.

EQUIPMENT

None

SAFETY

Take all spotting and lifting precautions.[76] Watch closely to assure gentle treatment of the bomb.

CONSIDER THIS

Does the group take time to make a plan? How do they physically support each other? Listen for ways strategies are introduced and implemented.

[76] See Spotting and Call-Response Sequence on page 40.

VARIATIONS

To add an element of urgency, making the explosive a time bomb that will go off in five minutes.

PERSONAL NOTES AND RE-VIEW

PLANE CRASH

ACTIVITY BRIEF

This is a fun role-playing game that takes some problem solving and physical skills.

1. Set up the scenario by explaining to participants that each person possesses a vital component of the cure for cancer or a plague, technology for an important bridge or machine, or some other idea you create. The plane they are in crashes. They all survive, but several (or all) have been injured.
2. They must all get away from the crash site before the plane explodes, which will kill anyone who isn't in the safe zone. They must *all* get away as a group. They can't leave anyone behind. Set up a safe zone about 20 to 30 yards away that the group must get to.
3. Role-play being in a plane, flying around the open field together, and making plane noises. When you—the pilot—yell "Crash!" the whole group falls and spreads out over a small area.
4. Give each person an injury or handicap.

• Make the best athlete of the group a quadriplegic.
• Have a person who talks a lot be the one who has his tongue ripped out and can't speak.
• Give others various broken limbs.
• Give a persuasive member of the group a concussion that makes her try to convince the rest of the group that the safe zone is dangerous and nobody should go there.

• Allow a quiet or introverted group member to have no (or minor) injuries.

• Take away one person's sense of smell just for fun.

EQUIPMENT
_ Imagination

_ An open space

_ Rope or orange safety cones to mark the safe zone

SAFETY
Pick the crash site carefully. Watch for how participants carry each other. Dragging is okay, but make sure they're gentle and considerate.

CONSIDER THIS
Do they focus on limitations or capabilities? How do they combine their disabilities to accomplish their goal? Were there any injuries they were glad they didn't have?

VARIATIONS
Increase the challenge by allowing them only one trip to the safe zone.

Add an element of urgency by saying the plane is going to explode in eight minutes.

PERSONAL NOTES AND RE-VIEW

MONSTER WALK

ACTIVITY BRIEF
Here's an interesting problem that calls on the creativity of the whole group to solve and requires everyone to interact. The group transforms itself into a monster.

1. A limited number of feet can touch the ground. Subtract two from the total number of people in the group to arrive at the total number of monster feet. (If the size of the group is larger, you can subtract more). For example, if you have a group of 10, subtract two and the monster will have 16 feet. Eight people must carry 10. Only feet can touch the ground.

2. The monster must travel between two points that you designate. Make the distance far enough to test them, but not so far that they become discouraged.

3. This monster cannot reproduce asexually.[77]

EQUIPMENT
_ A marker to designate the distance the monster must walk

SAFETY
Make sure the group doesn't stack people too high. Don't let them drag any monster parts (people).

CONSIDER THIS
Who steps into leadership? How do they assume leadership? How are ideas managed and implemented? Does the group label anyone by gender or size? How do people handle failure and frustration?

VARIATIONS
You can repeat this activity with diminishing numbers of feet. Start with enough feet so only a few group members need to be carried. After each successful monster walk, take away a few feet. Notice how the strategies change as the resources diminish.

PERSONAL NOTES AND RE-VIEW

TRAFFIC JAM

ACTIVITY BRIEF
This simple puzzle can frustrate even the most advanced groups.

Figure 2-1
Traffic Jam

1. Set out the carpet squares in a straight line.

2. Arrange everyone on one square with the open space in the middle. The people on one end face the group on the other end.

3. The object is to have the participants on each half move to the other half, using only legal moves.

Legal moves

1. A person may move into an empty space in front of him.

2. A person may move around one person *facing him* into an empty space.

Illegal moves

1. A person may not move backward.

2. A person may not move around someone facing the same direction.

3. A person may not move into an empty space behind him.

EQUIPMENT

_ Carpet squares—or paper or backpacks or other item to designate the available spots—one for each person plus one

SAFETY

Physically there is little risk. You may have to manage the emotional safety of the group as the frustration builds.

CONSIDER THIS

How many times does the group repeat the same mistake? Does the group ever impose additional rules on itself?[78] What was it like to be in the middle? What was it like to be on an end? Notice that movement is often possible even after a mistake.

VARIATIONS

After the team has completed the puzzle once, their order will be reversed. Have them repeat the exercise from their new positions.

Increase the challenge by having them solve the challenge without talking.

PERSONAL NOTES AND RE-VIEW

[78] A self-imposed rule might be, "Never move so two people facing the same way are together."

ACID RIVER

ACTIVITY BRIEF

Problem solving, communication, and a difficult physical challenge are all part of this activity. Before starting this activity, check the setup to make sure there is at least one solution.

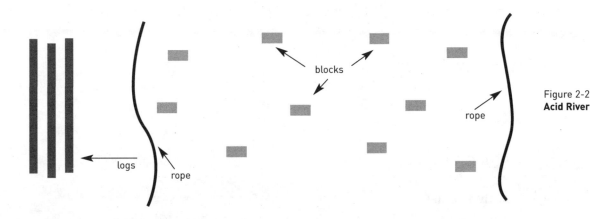

Figure 2-2
Acid River

1. The group encounters a river of wicked acid.
2. The entire group must get across using only the logs available (three 8-foot boards).
3. They can use the rocks (strategically placed) in the river.
4. They can't touch the acid; otherwise the whole group must start over.
5. The logs can touch but only for a limited time, say one second.

EQUIPMENT

Often this activity is a permanent feature at a low-element challenge course. Portable kits are available, or you can make your own.

_ 3 eight- to ten-foot 4"x4" beams or peeler poles for logs
_ Bricks, cinder blocks, or six-inch lengths of 2"x4" boards for river rocks
_ 2 lengths of rope to define the river banks

SAFETY

Be sure the playing surface is level and free of holes. Be sure the group is careful as they pass around the logs. Encourage them to lift with their legs and to be aware of both ends as the logs move.[79]

CONSIDER THIS

Does the group take time to plan? Do they work as a team or as individuals or in smaller groups? Who steps into leadership? Does the leadership transfer to others at all? How do they handle failure and frustration?

VARIATIONS

Give the group some useful props to see how they handle extraneous material. Do

[79] No Three Stooges head bonks!

they find uses for any of it? Ignore it?

See Sea of Trolls below for another twist.

PERSONAL NOTES AND RE-VIEW

SEA OF TROLLS

ACTIVITY BRIEF

This activity is similar to Acid River (page 63) but with added elements to increase the challenge. Before starting this activity, check the setup to make sure there is at least one solution.

Figure 2-3
Sea of Trolls

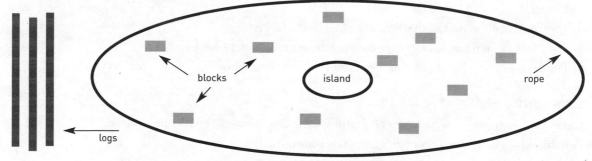

1. The group encounters a sea that is guarded by nasty trolls. (See the diagram.)
2. The entire group must get to the island using only the logs available and the troll's trash.
3. They can use the rocks in the river.
4. They must retrieve the troll treasure and return to the shore by another route.
5. If anyone or anything touches the surface of the sea, the trolls become angry and punish the offender. Punishments handed out by the head troll—you—may range from having the whole group start over to giving the offender troll trash to carry.

EQUIPMENT

_ 3 eight- to ten-foot 4"x4" beams or peeler poles for logs
_ Bricks, cinder blocks, or six-inch lengths of 2"x4" boards for river rocks—strategically placed
_ 1 or more lengths of rope to define the island
_ A big box or blow-up toy (that's not too heavy) to use as the troll treasure
_ Random junk to use as troll trash

SAFETY

Be sure the playing surface is level and free from holes. Be sure the group is careful as they pass around the logs. Encourage them to lift with their legs and to be aware of both ends as the logs move.[80]

CONSIDER THIS

Does the group take time to plan? Do they work as a team or as individuals or in smaller groups? Who steps into leadership? Does the leadership transfer to others at all? How do they handle failure and frustration?

VARIATIONS

This activity works well with multiple groups. Let each group have its own set of logs. They can compete or cooperate.

PERSONAL NOTES AND RE-VIEW

MACHINE

ACTIVITY BRIEF

This activity combines physical motion with social and interpersonal risk.

1. Have the group form a circle.
2. Explain that the group is going to become a machine. Everyone will function as a part.
3. Ask for a volunteer. He creates a simple repetitive (nonvulgar) motion and a sound to go with it. The volunteer steps into the middle of the circle and performs this motion and sound.
4. The rest of the group members join in—whenever they're ready—with different repetitive motions and sounds that link to the machine. Have everyone keep synchronized.

EQUIPMENT

None

SAFETY

No physical safety concerns, but be sure to maintain an emotionally and socially safe environment.

[80] No Three Stooges head bonks!

CONSIDER THIS

For some people this is a simple activity without much risk. For others it's terrifying. What are the challenges in this activity? How does it feel to be the first one in the middle? Why do some people jump in right away and others hang back or not jump in at all?

VARIATIONS

Have the machine increase or decrease speed. Give the machine a specific product to produce before the group starts or ask afterward what the machine does.

PERSONAL NOTES AND RE-VIEW

STOP AND CONNECT

ACTIVITY BRIEF

You'll be surprised at how powerful and revealing this simple activity can be.

1. Have the group spread out in a large open area.
2. Have the participants walk around, focusing on how they are walking and their own thoughts.
3. When you call out "Stop and connect," everyone stops moving completely and makes eye contact with one other person nearby. The object is to connect with that person without words or gestures.[81]
4. There might be some nervous laughter but encourage a quiet atmosphere. The quieter it is, the more powerful the experience.
5. After a little while (long enough to be uncomfortable), call out "Continue." Everyone starts walking again.
6. Repeat this several times so that each person can connect with a few people.

EQUIPMENT

_ A large, open area

SAFETY

There isn't much physical risk. Be aware of the interpersonal intensity that results from holding eye contact with another person.

[81] Connecting isn't just staring at another person until your eyeballs dry out. It's more about giving each other undivided attention and seeing what happens.

CONSIDER THIS

Participants will laugh, but try to get them to go beyond laughter. What else might be there? What is the challenge of this activity? How did they interpret "connecting" with others? Did they find some people easier to connect with than others?

VARIATIONS

Before continuing, have participants introduce themselves to their eye-contact partner.

Give the group something to notice while they are connected, for example, what their partners might teach them or how they might help each other.

PERSONAL NOTES AND RE-VIEW

WOUNDED COMMUNITY

ACTIVITY BRIEF

Wounded Community creates a powerful atmosphere by asking people to consider their own woundedness and those of others in the group.

1. Give people a few minutes to think about how they have been wounded in the past—physical wounds like broken bones or emotional wounds such as disrespect or insults.
2. Challenge them to portray their wounds in simple, repetitive motions—a broken leg might limp, a broken heart might be hands clutching a chest.
3. Let them spread out and reflect for a few minutes.
4. After they have thought about this, ask for volunteers to do the physical motion they have connected to their wounds. Select about a third of the group.
5. Get everyone's attention and explain that they will be doing a silent activity. A few members of their community are wounded.
6. If they haven't been asked to show their wound, they're healthy.
7. Healthy people take on the wounded person's ailment by walking silently next to them and copying the movement exactly. The wounded person is healed if she feels the healthy person is copying the wounded movement exactly. Wounded people should not give up their wounds until the person taking it really understands it.

8. Once the wounded person feels the other is accurately copying the motion, they are no longer wounded. They are then free to walk around normally and take on another's wound.

Silence is important. Allow the group a good amount of time to explore their own woundedness and to explore others' wounds as well. This can be an incredibly powerful event.

EQUIPMENT
None

SAFETY
Physically this is not a risky activity, but it can be scary emotionally. While encouraging the group members to go deep, allow them to choose how deep they want to go. Don't force them to explore emotionally painful wounds if they aren't willing to do so on their own. Let them use a broken arm if their broken heart is too recent or too painful.

CONSIDER THIS
How do they handle being healthy when others are wounded? How do they handle another person's wounds? Were there wounds that scared them? Did they not want to give up a wound? What was it like to have someone take their wounds from them?

VARIATIONS
Do this activity with groups that have developed trust and rapport. It shouldn't be done if the group members can't take it seriously. Try Stop and Connect (page 66) first. If they can handle that activity, they are more likely be able to take Wounded Community seriously as well.

PERSONAL NOTES AND RE-VIEW

HELIUM STICK

ACTIVITY BRIEF

1. Show the team the specially developed rod filled with helium (okay, it's really a tent pole, but you don't have to tell them that), which you're holding horizontally. Have each person place only one index finger under the rod so that together the group is supporting the rod horizontally at eye level.[82]

82 It works best if there are some people on each side of the stick, but you can let the group members decide where they'll stand.

2. The index finger must remain perfectly horizontal and cannot touch any other finger.

3. They can't bend or tilt the index finger.

4. They are to set the rod on the ground.

Continuously remind the group that everyone must be touching the stick at all times and that they must keep their fingers straight and level.

EQUIPMENT

_ A very light stick—Graphite tent poles work well.

SAFETY

None

CONSIDER THIS

Why is this so difficult?

VARIATIONS

Use a hula-hoop instead of a stick.

PERSONAL NOTES AND RE-VIEW

KEYPAD

ACTIVITY BRIEF

Create a story—perhaps a spy or save-the-world scenario—to go along with this challenge. Set up the keypad as shown in the diagram. Don't let the group see the keypad before their first attempt.

Figure 2-4
Keypad

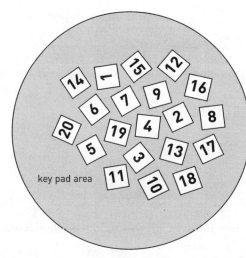

1. The group members must all start at the designated spot, which is both the start and finish lines.
2. Time the group to see how quickly they can go to the keypad, touch all the keys[83] in sequence, and return to the starting point.
3. Time starts when the first person crosses the start line.
4. Only one person can enter the keypad area at a time. Each number can only be touched once and only by one person.
5. The time stops when the last person crosses the finish line.
6. Give the group several tries and a time limit to get their best time—five tries in 10 minutes or seven tries in 15 minutes.

EQUIPMENT
_ 1 rope for the start and finish line
_ 1 long rope to define the keypad area
_ 20 keys with the numbers 1 to 20 on them—The keys can be anything from commercial markers to carpet samples to paper plates.
_ An open area

SAFETY
Make sure the area you choose is free from tripping hazards like holes, sprinklers, or rocks. Avoid wet grass or other slippery surfaces as well.

CONSIDER THIS
Do group members spend time planning before they've seen the keypad? Do they make a plan based on real information or guesses? They'll ask you questions, many of which are how-to or can-we questions rather than clarification of the rules. Try to only clarify the rules and not give solutions. Do they try one idea several times, or do they try several ideas?

VARIATIONS
Without telling the group, take away two or three numbers late in the sequence. What they do when they can't find 15 or 18?

PERSONAL NOTES AND RE-VIEW

---

[83] The keys are the 1 to 20 markers.

UNFINISHED BRIDGE

ACTIVITY BRIEF

At first the group may think this is an impossible task. With a little thought and cooperation, they can figure out a solution.

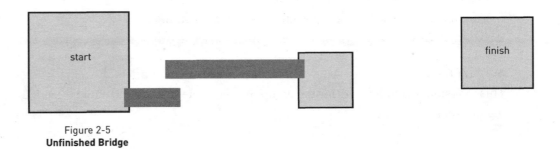

Figure 2-5
Unfinished Bridge

1. The group finds three platforms of different sizes and two boards.
2. Using only the two boards given, the group must move from the first platform to the last without the boards or themselves touching the ground.
3. Neither board by itself can reach the other platforms, and one board is significantly shorter than the other.

The solution involves counterbalancing using a simple lever.

EQUIPMENT

This crossing activity is often found as a permanent event on low-challenge courses. Portable sets can be purchased,[84] or you can make the pieces.

_ 3 platforms, 2'x2', 3'x3', and 5'x5'. The platforms should be three to five inches off the ground.
_ 1 eight-foot 2"x6" plank
_ 1 five-foot 2"x6" plank

SAFETY

Be sure the group is careful as they pass boards back and forth. Do not allow jumping from platform to platform or using the planks as diving boards. Stop unsafe behavior before anyone tries it.

CONSIDER THIS

This activity involves a bit of creative thinking and simple physics. Listen for the way the group processes ideas. Solutions may also involve repetitive actions. Look for mistakes made because participants lack focus.

VARIATIONS

Increase the urgency by giving a time limit. Increase the difficulty by giving the team a bucket of water to bring along without spilling it.

[84] See Resources on page 152.

GROUP JUMP ROPE

ACTIVITY BRIEF

This is a simple and fun way for the group to coordinate actions and explore working together.

1. Give the group a long piece of rope and choose two volunteers to twirl the rope.
2. Offer several jump rope challenges:

_ Run through the rope twirling full circle without jumping.
_ Adding one person at a time, see how many people the group can get jumping at one time.
_ See if they can get everyone, including the rope twirlers, jumping at the same time.
_ Have the whole group pass through the twirling rope at one time, doing one and only one jump as they pass through.

EQUIPMENT

_ 1 rope at least 25 feet long—The length depends on the number of people in the group.

SAFETY

Be sure the surface is open and free of hazards. Make sure the twirlers don't turn the rope too fast.

CONSIDER THIS

Some people are better jumpers than others. How do people encourage one another? How do they act toward people who mess up? Do they take time to make a plan?

VARIATIONS

Try the challenges with the rope swinging from side to side rather than full circle.

PERSONAL NOTES AND RE-VIEW

THROUGH THE BOX

ACTIVITY BRIEF
The group needs to employ strategic thinking and trust to complete this task.

1. Use PVC tubes and connectors to make a hollow cube.
2. Balance the box by one corner on a stand.[85]
3. The first participant enters through one side and exits using a different side.
4. Everyone in the group must pass through the box without touching it or knocking it off its stand—and no one can use the same entrance-exit combination.

EQUIPMENT
_ 1 plastic pot or a mug or round storage container, 5 to 6 inches in diameter
_ Through the Box requires a kit[86] or a bunch of PVC pipes and connectors assembled into a cube.

or

_ 24 pieces of PVC, each 18 inches long
_ 8 three-way PVC connectors (one side threaded)
_ 12 PVC joiners

SAFETY
This event may involve lifting and carrying. Be sure to review proper spotting techniques on page 40. Do *not* allow any diving or jumping through the box.

CONSIDER THIS
Do they start with the end in mind? Do they use the openings strategically? How do they support each other?

VARIATIONS
Make other rules about the openings they may use, how the openings can be combined, and how many times they may use an opening to increase the difficulty.

Give them an object that they must take with them through the box. Make them stay connected or touching until everyone is through the box.

PERSONAL NOTES AND RE-VIEW

[85] Use a small plastic flower pot or round storage container.

[86] You can purchase a Cube kit through a challenge course company. See Resources on page 152.

CARABINEER WEB

ACTIVITY BRIEF

Combine learning names with a challenge.

1. Have the group stand in a circle shoulder to shoulder.
2. Give one person the rope. This person say his own name and asks the name of a person across the circle. He hands the leading end of the rope to the second person and continues to hold the end of the rope loosely.
3. The second person repeats the process by saying her own name and asking another person's name as she hands off the leading edge of the rope. This handoff must go over the rope that already crosses the circle.
4. Repeat the process. The next pass must go under the other lines. Continue until everyone is holding loosely to part of the rope once.
5. The last person passes the rope to the person who began the web, which is now complete.
6. Clip a carabineer to the rope where the first person is holding it.
7. The group passes the carabineer down the line until it comes off the other end. The group can't touch the carabineer or let go of the rope.

EQUIPMENT

_ 1 carabineer
_ 1 50-foot thin rope or cord for 10 to 12 people

SAFETY

Have the participants hold the rope loosely so they don't get rope burns.

CONSIDER THIS

This activity works well at the start of a group's process. It helps them learn names and creates a safe way for them to begin to work together.

VARIATIONS

After they pass the carabineer around the web, see if they can untangle the web without letting go of the cord.

Increase the challenge by asking them to put a simple knot in the rope between each person without letting go of the rope.

PERSONAL NOTES AND RE-VIEW

DUCK RINGS

ACTIVITY BRIEF

1. Place the cup on the ground. Set the center of the duck ring[87] on top of the cup with all the strings stretched out on the ground around it. Balance the orange on the ring on top of the cup.
2. The group must lift the orange by the duck ring strings and carry it around a series of obstacles and replace it on the cup.
3. The team can touch only the ends of the strings. Once a participant picks up a string, he can't switch the hand holding it.
4. The orange can touch only the ring. No one can wrap it onto the ring with the strings. If the orange drops, the group must start over.

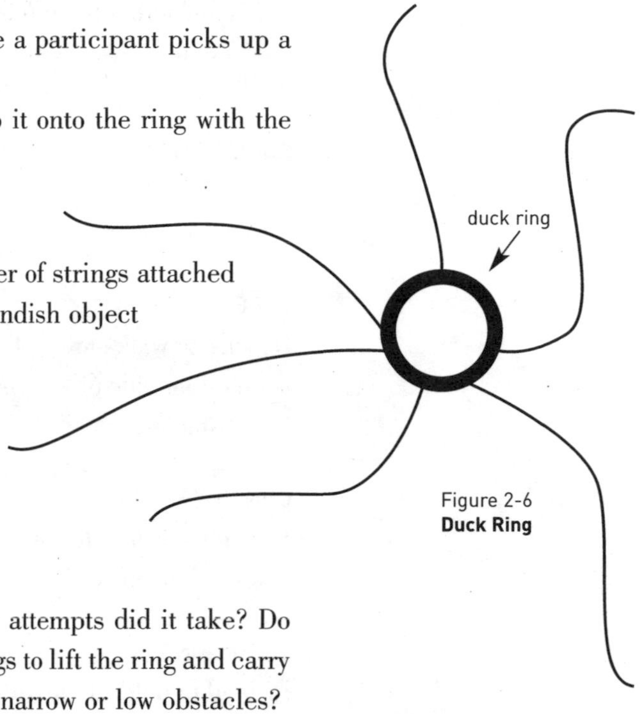

EQUIPMENT

_ 1 duck ring—a two-inch ring of duct tape with a number of strings attached
_ 1 orange—or tennis ball, wad of duct tape, or other roundish object
_ 1 cup
_ Obstacles to move around, through, over, and under

SAFETY

Be sure the area is free of hazards.

CONSIDER THIS

How difficult is it to first pick up the object? How many attempts did it take? Do they try to balance the object or create tension in the strings to lift the ring and carry the object? How do they manage to go through or around narrow or low obstacles?

VARIATIONS

Just before the group returns the object to it's starting point, give them a hula-hoop or a loop of webbing. Tell them they must pass the object through it without letting go of their strings.

PERSONAL NOTES AND RE-VIEW

duck ring

Figure 2-6
Duck Ring

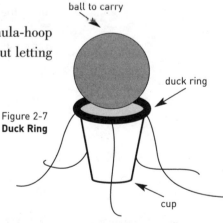

ball to carry

duck ring

Figure 2-7
Duck Ring

cup

[87] This is a variation of an activity called Bull Rings. I found myself without a metal ring to make a bull ring, so I made a loop out of duct tape and put an orange on it. There you have it. The birth of Duck Rings.

SHERPA WALK

ACTIVITY BRIEF

If you need to get your group from one place to another, this is a fun way to turn it into a challenge.

1. Have the group either put on blindfolds or close their eyes.
2. Have them find each other and form a chain. Or you can lay a rope on the ground and have them find and hold on to it.
3. Take the front end and lead them on an adventure.

EQUIPMENT

_ Blindfolds, one for each person (optional)
_ Rope (optional)

SAFETY

Be sure to walk slowly. The end of the line tends to cut corners, so be aware of what is on either side of your path as you walk. Warn the first person in line of approaching obstacles.

CONSIDER THIS

How does it feel to lose vision? Do the people in front warn the people in back of potential obstacles? How do the group members communicate with each other?

VARIATIONS

Instead of holding the rope or holding the lead person's hand, try leading the group with voice commands only or just a sound such as clapping hands or clacking two rocks together.

PERSONAL NOTES AND RE-VIEW

BLINDFOLD ADVENTURE

ACTIVITY BRIEF

This activity allows the group to explore trust and the use of senses other than vision.

1. Have the group pair up. One person wears a blindfold, and the other is the guide.
2. The guides leads their partners on adventures by running on flat, smooth, soft surface; climbing large rocks; introducing them to a tree that they have to find when they take the blindfolds off; and whatever other creative ideas they can come up with.

EQUIPMENT

_ Blindfolds, enough for at least half the group

SAFETY

Be sure the guides understand they're responsible for their partners' safety. Do *not* allow them to go onto roads or parking lots.

CONSIDER THIS

What's it like to be blind? Was the end of the adventure different from the beginning? How did they use their other senses? Did the guide do anything that made them less safe? More safe? How did the guide build trust? What was it like to be responsible for the safety of others?

VARIATIONS

Allow the guides to use only voice or only touch to lead their partners.

PERSONAL NOTES AND RE-VIEW

CAMERA

ACTIVITY BRIEF

This exercise helps participants see through another's eyes.

1. Have the group pair up. One person in each pair wears a blindfold and acts as the camera. The other person is the photographer.
2. Have each pair agree on a signal that activates the camera's shutter—perhaps a tap on the shoulder or a tug on the ear.
3. The photographer takes the camera on a photo safari and shoots a small roll of film (about four shots). When the camera gets the shutter signal, he lifts the blindfold for one second and pulls it down again.

4. Encourage the photographer to be intentional about the pictures she takes. She should choose a theme for the pictures. Closeups are interesting and challenging.

5. After the roll of film has been shot, have the camera explain the photos and guess the theme.

6. Switch roles.

EQUIPMENT
_ Blindfolds for at least half the group

SAFETY
Stress the importance of the cameras' safety to the photographers. Do *not* allow them to go onto any roads or parking lots.

CONSIDER THIS
What was it like as the camera to figure out what the picture was supposed to be? How difficult was it for the photographer to try get the ideas across? What were their favorite pictures?

VARIATIONS
Instead of allowing the photographers to choose their own themes, assign the theme based on lessons you're teaching.

PERSONAL NOTES AND RE-VIEW

SPIDER'S WEB

ACTIVITY BRIEF
This activity involves strategy, trust, and a physical challenge. The Spider's Web is part of many permanent low-challenge courses, but you can easily tie one yourself. Introduce this activity in the context of a story: A giant spider lives in the tree and, when her web is touched, she comes down and eats the intruders.[88]

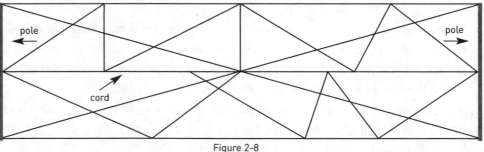

Figure 2-8
Spider's Web

88 Use your imagination to embellish this story or invent your own.

Gather the group on one side of the spider's web.

Everyone must get through the web without touching any of the strings.

Each hole in the web can be used only once.

If anyone touches the web, the whole team must start over.

People act as spotters when they're not going through the web.

EQUIPMENT

_ Cord or string, enough to make the spider web, or a purchased web

_ 2 trees or poles

SAFETY

As with all lifting activities, be sure the group knows how to spot and lift safely. (See page 40.) *No diving or jumping!* Allow a few people to be on the far side of the web to act as spotters, but don't let them help pass people through the web. Once a few people are safely through, those spotters can return so they can pass through the web as well.

CONSIDER THIS

Does the group start with the end in mind? Do they allow people to choose their own hole in the web or do they assign them? How do they solve the problems of getting the first and last person through?

VARIATIONS

If this too difficult at first, allow them to come into contact with the string three times before the whole team has to start over.

To increase the difficulty give them an object to carry when they go through the web or make them stay connected as they pass through.

PERSONAL NOTES AND RE-VIEW

NITRO CROSSING

ACTIVITY BRIEF

This is another popular activity found at many low-challenge course facilities. Nitro Crossing should be constructed and maintained by a professional.[89]

89 See Resources on page 152.

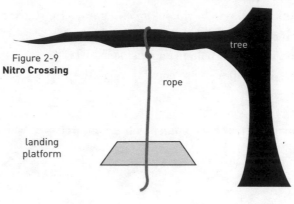

Figure 2-9
Nitro Crossing

tree

rope

landing
platform

start here

1. Gather the group at the riverbank. They must find a way to get the group across the river along with a container of nitroglycerin[90] without spilling any of it.
2. Start with the rope hanging in the middle. Make the group figure out how to get it.
3. The entire group must stay on the landing platform, which has limited space.
4. If someone touches the river, the whole group has to start over.

EQUIPMENT
_ 1 Nitro Crossing site, professionally constructed

SAFETY
Do not tie a loop in the rope or allow anyone to wrap the rope around their hands, fingers, or wrists. Never allow feet to get higher than the person's waist.

Allow a few members of the group to be on the other side of the river to act as spotters until a few people make the crossing. Then have them return so they can cross themselves.

CONSIDER THIS
What are the challenges inherent in this activity? Who steps up as a leader? How does the group decide on a plan? Do the leaders listen to all the ideas offered? How does the group address the varying physical abilities of the participants?

VARIATIONS
To assure that no one steps on or over the line, balance a board or a stick on two blocks. Penalize the group if anyone knocks it off.

PERSONAL NOTES AND RE-VIEW

[90] Water can do a mean imitation of several vital liquids. Choose a different one, if you like.

HA!

ACTIVITY BRIEF

1. Have one person lie down on the ground. The next person puts his head on the stomach of the first person. The next person puts her head on the second. The pattern continues until everyone is lying on the ground.

2. The object is to say "Ha!" without laughing or making any other sound. The first person says "Ha!" once, the second person says it twice, the third person says it three times, and so, on until the last person takes a turn.

3. If anyone laughs, talks, snickers, or makes any other sound than "Ha!" the whole group starts over.

EQUIPMENT

None

SAFETY

Be aware of stomach pain from laughing too hard.

CONSIDER THIS

Does anyone get frustrated? Is there tension between people who are having fun and people who want to finish the task?

VARIATIONS

To increase the challenge, make the group go down the line and back again. Or give them a funny-sounding two-syllable word to say instead. I've used *shooter* and *gower*. Look for words that make the chest or belly move when said loud and forcefully.

PERSONAL NOTES AND RE-VIEW

HUMAN SCULPTURE

ACTIVITY BRIEF

While most initiatives offer physical and intellectual challenges, this one works mostly on a social-interpersonal level.

1. Divide into groups of three. One person is the clay; two are the artists.
2. Toss out a topic, for example, a baseball game, a movie theater, or Thanksgiving.
3. The artists sculpt their vision of the concept out of the clay. They can talk to each other but not to the clay. They physically move the clay into the desired position. Remind them to include facial expressions.
4. Repeat the task several times, allowing others to be the clay.

EQUIPMENT
None

SAFETY
Be sure to keep an emotionally safe environment.

CONSIDER THIS
What's it like for the clay to be totally controlled by the artist? How do the various groups interpret the same theme?

VARIATIONS
Have themes progress from concrete to abstract ideas, such as freedom, justice, and fear.

PERSONAL NOTES AND RE-VIEW

Small Group Activities and Exercises

Chapter 2.2

Getting people to interact in a small group setting can be a challenge, especially if they don't know each other well. These exercises create opportunities to explore interesting issues and encourage individuals to contribute their feelings and insight to the group. This diverse collection offers a sampling of ideas to promote communication and to create an interactive environment. The key is to focus on the interaction of the group members.

JUNGLE ISLAND

Break into groups of three to five (although you can have as many as 10). This exercise nearly runs itself once you've given out the first handout.

Give the group Salvageable Resources (page 91) and 15 to 20 minutes to select the resources they'll salvage from the ship. When they're ready to move to the next stage, give them Island Resources (page 92), a large piece of paper, and markers. Don't let them look at Island Resources until they've completed their list of salvaged items. Allow them about 20 minutes to work on their escape plan.

When they're finished, give each group a chance to present their island and plans.

EQUIPMENT
_ Copies of Salvageable Resources (page 91), one for each person
_ Copies of Island Resources (page 92), one for each person
_ Butcher paper or a flip chart
_ Markers or pens

CONSIDER THIS
As the groups are discussing their resources and plans, listen to how they go about making their decisions. How do leaders emerge? Look for creativity and the way it's expressed. This activity is a good way to establish how a group sets priorities.

VALUES AUCTION

Give each person a values auction sheet. Let them have about 10 minutes to complete this exercise individually.

Gather participants into one or more small groups. The group members must reach a consensus about what they will bid on and how much they are willing to spend. If you have several groups, you can hold the auction. If you have one group, discuss the reasons they made their selections and what makes something valuable.

EQUIPMENT
_ Copies of Values Auction (page 93)
_ Pens

PERSONAL NOTES AND RE-VIEW

LONG RANGE, SHORT RANGE

In this exercise, the group needs to make some tough decisions about how to use resources. This exercise creates tension between immediate needs and long-range planning. Give everyone a copy of and a pen.

EQUIPMENT
_ Copies of Long Range, Short Range (page 94)
_ Pens

PERSONAL NOTES AND RE-VIEW

COPY MACHINE

Communication can be complicated. This exercise shows just how difficult clear communication can be.

Before the group meets, draw a simple pattern on a piece of paper. Make enough copies of this pattern for half the group.[91] Also have plenty of blank paper for the other half of the group and pens.

Have the group members pair up and sit back to back. Tell them that each pair is now a copy machine. Give one person the original without letting the other see it (they can choose who will play which part). The person with the original has 10 minutes to describe what she sees—only with words—so her partner can draw an exact copy.

EQUIPMENT
_ Copies of a simple pattern, one for each group
_ Blank paper, several sheets for each group
_ Pens, one for each group

CONSIDER THIS
How close were the copies to the originals? How did people describe the parts of the pattern? What made this activity difficult? What was confusing? What strategies were helpful?

PERSONAL NOTES AND RE-VIEW

[91] You can create more than one pattern if you want to.

FEELINGS TOSS

Sometimes people just need an excuse to share their feelings. After a group has developed some trust and connection, try this exercise.

Gather the group into a circle and toss in a tossable object. Whoever has the object has the opportunity to share one word that describes how she or he is feeling about the day, the week, the theme, or recent topics of group discussion.

This is a useful way to check on perceptions of how the group is doing.

EQUIPMENT
_ 1 tossable object

PERSONAL NOTES AND RE-VIEW

WEATHER REPORT

Some people have trouble putting their feelings or attitudes into words. Weather Report gives them a creative way to talk about how they're doing and what they're feeling after an activity or a particularly intense discussion.

Ask the group members to describe how they're feeling in the form of a weather report. Be sure to give them a few minutes to gather their thoughts and compose the report. Go around the circle and give them the opportunity to share their weather reports. Let them know they have the option to pass but encourage everyone to give it a try.

This exercise can lead to an open discussion of the group members' feelings and attitudes, but let it develop naturally.

EQUIPMENT
None

PERSONAL NOTES AND RE-VIEW

TALKING STICK

A talking stick doesn't have to be an actual stick. Any object that can be passed from person to person works. What makes the object special is the role it plays in a group discussion. If a group, in general, talks too much or too little, a talking stick can help improve communication.

Choose an interesting object to be the talking stick. Inform the group that when the talking stick is in the group the attention and focus of the group follows the stick. Whoever has the stick has the attention and focus of the group. That person is the only one who can talk. When that person is finished talking, he gets to choose who holds the stick next.

It can be given to a person who has her hand out, indicating she has something to say, or it can be given to someone the stick-holder asks a question of.

EQUIPMENT

_ 1 talking stick or other object

PERSONAL NOTES AND RE-VIEW

THREE ROCKS

This exercise helps people think about what they have to say before they say it.

Before a discussion or an exercise let the group know that they will have to pay to talk. Have people find three small rocks each,[92] which they must pay you to talk.

They may not give their rocks away or take rocks from anyone else. Once they are out of rocks, they remain silent until the end of the activity or discussion. The exercise is not over until everyone has spent all of his rocks.

EQUIPMENT

_ 3 rocks (or other objects) per person

PERSONAL NOTES AND RE-VIEW

[92] Or leaves, pieces of paper, or pens. You can also allow more than three items.

THIS OR THAT

It can be fun to discover what people think about a variety of topics. In this activity, the group chooses between two items. They must choose one or the other; there is no middle ground.

Before the group meets, make a This or That list. The list can start off with lighthearted choices like Froot Loops or Coco-Puffs and Snickers or Three Musketeers. Let the topics get increasingly personal and deep, until you're offering choices such as safety or freedom, justice or harmony, options or conclusions, honesty or compassion.

Participants will make their choices known by moving to one designated area or another. Once they have chosen an area, have them observe who voted with them and who voted for the other choice. Don't rush through the list. Give the group members a few moments to let the situation sink in.

EQUIPMENT
_ List of choices

PERSONAL NOTES AND RE-VIEW

HAVE YOU EVER...?

This exercise gives people an opportunity to reveal information about themselves in a safe way—by answering "Have you ever…?" questions.

Before the activity begins, write up a list of questions. Start off with light information: Have you ever water skied, been rock climbing, fought with your siblings? Move toward personal and significant topics. Have you ever been kissed, been made fun of, witnessed to a stranger, shoplifted, had your heart broken?

When the group meets, have everyone stand side by side behind a line. Explain that you're going to ask a series of questions. If the question applies to them, they should step over the line *when you tell them to*.[93] After you ask a question, wait a few seconds before you tell them to respond to give them time to make their choice. Ask them to notice who stepped out with them and who didn't. Have them step back and move on to the next question.

As the questions get more intense, they'll need more time to let the experience impact them. This activity is powerful if you ask the right questions.

[93] It's important that they all step at the same time so their responses aren't influenced by their peers. You want genuine responses. You can have them close their eyes until they step out.

EQUIPMENT
_ List of questions

PERSONAL NOTES AND RE-VIEW

CLAY FIGURES

Some people are verbal and love to talk. Others need a little help. Clay Figures helps people who are less verbal to express themselves.

Give each person in the group a lump of clay[94] and a topic to sculpt. Good topics involve self-perception: How do you think people see you? How do you want to be seen? What do you want to grow into?

The expressions can be self-portraits, but emphasize they can also be symbols, perhaps a big hand to represent wanting to be helpful, a broken coffee mug to represent being a broken vessel in need of grace, or a manger to represent needing rest.

EQUIPMENT
_ Clay
_ A list of topics

PERSONAL NOTES AND RE-VIEW

[94] Modeling clay and Play-doh work well. Silly Putty works great as well and doesn't dry out.

AFFIRMATION BEADS

Sometimes it's a good idea to create a formal excuse for people to encourage one another. Before the group meets, go to a craft store and buy some cheap beads and a spool of string.

When the group meets, give each person a piece of string and at least as many beads as participants. Ask them to hold the beads in one hand and the string in the other.

Have them think about how the others individually have positively impacted their lives. What have they done? How have they helped? Give the group about five minutes to think.

Have them walk around the room, giving out beads and sharing encouragements about how they have been affected. The interactions should be positive and personal. As they receive beads from others, they thread them onto their own strings. The strings can be made into bracelets or key-chains so participants remember their value when they see them.

EQUIPMENT

_ Beads, enough so each participant can give one (or more) to every other person
_ String, long enough to tie around wrists, one piece for each person

PERSONAL NOTES AND RE-VIEW

JUNGLE ISLAND
SALVAGEABLE RESOURCES

You've just been shipwrecked somewhere in the South Pacific. Fortunately everyone is able to make it to an island. You're able to even salvage items from your ship to help you survive. Given the list of resources available to you, decide as a group what you will bring with you to the island. Then decide what you'll do with these resources to survive and get rescued from Jungle Island.

You are only able to salvage 20 of the following items from the ship. (Two chickens are available. If you take both chickens, you've taken two items.)

Do not look at the second handout until you've finished choosing the items you're salvaging.

_____ 2 chickens
_____ 2 roosters
_____ 3 barrels of crude oil
_____ 3 coils of rope, 100 feet each
_____ 5 pulleys
_____ 1 set of pots and pans
_____ 2 trunks filled with old clothes
_____ 5 boxes of matches
_____ 1 Xbox
_____ 2 complete sails
_____ 1 shredded sail
_____ 5 vinyl mattresses
_____ 3 bottles of insect repellent
_____ 10 rubber rain coats
_____ 2 inner tubes
_____ 1 map of the Pacific Ocean
_____ 4 barrels of fresh water, 33 gallons each
_____ 1 box of flares (no flare gun)
_____ 3 packages of beef, 5 pounds each
_____ 3 butane-powered curling irons (full of butane)
_____ 1 compass
_____ 8 six-packs of Coke
_____ 4 bottles of sunscreen
_____ 15 Bibles

When you have decided on the resources, continue with the next handout, Island Resources.

JUNGLE ISLAND
ISLAND RESOURCES

Below is a list of what you find on the island. Draw a picture of the island that includes all these things on the paper your facilitator provides you. Given all that you find on the island and the items you have salvaged from the boat, make a rescue plan. Use the picture to show how you'll use the salvaged items from the boat.

You can draw, write, or list your plan on the paper provided. Be creative and have fun!

1 island, fully equipped with dirt and blood-sucking bugs

1 sandy beach

1 grove of mango trees

Did I mention the blood-sucking bugs?

1 accessible lagoon-like inlet

1 huge banyan tree

Rocky cliffs

15 banana trees

40 wild man-eating pigs, with big nasty teeth

1 grove of coconut trees

Lots of mango-eating rats

Flocks of wild birds

25 rabid banana-eating bats

1 small freshwater spring (which produces about 1/2 gallon of

water per person per day)

Don't forget the blood-sucking bugs

VALUES AUCTION

Suppose that the items below could actually be purchased with money and that you have been given $150,000 to spend at this auction.

   Decide how much money you are willing to pay for each item listed below. You must spend all the money, and once you have allocated an amount to one item, it cannot be transferred to another item. Decide how much you are willing to spend on each item. These items will go to the highest bidder. Use this sheet to help you decide which items to bid on and how much you want to bid.

_____ Honesty

_____ Achievement

_____ Justice

_____ Wealth

_____ Love

_____ Power

_____ Peace

_____ Joy

_____ Health

_____ Beauty

_____ Happiness

_____ Knowledge

_____ Recognition

_____ Religion

_____ Pleasure

_____ Freedom

_____ Wisdom

_____ Altruism

_____ Discipline

_____ Patience

_____ Total

LONG RANGE, SHORT RANGE

We have six fully grown trees on our land. We have no other trees around our house or anywhere else on our land. We need firewood for cooking and to keep warm. We need to decide how best to use our trees.

What will be the best action to take?

Consider these questions:

What will happen next summer when it's hot?

What about the next winter when we need more firewood?

What problems might there be for animals?

What can we do to meet our immediate needs and our needs in the future?

Large Group Activities and Exercises

Large group activities can be used to help students learn and grow as well as those designed for small groups. You may need to break down barriers to show the group they can do the impossible. Or you may simply want to divide a large group into several smaller groups or to generate energy. Here are some ideas to help you be experiential with large groups.

THWACKER TAG

You may need to generate laughter at the beginning of a meeting or energy after a break. Use Thwacker Tag[95] to accomplish this in a lively way.

Identify clear boundaries on the field and make sure everyone knows where they are. Choose five[96] volunteers to be It. Toss the thwackers into the middle of the field. The people who are It use the thwackers to thwack—tag—the others. Once It thwacks someone, he tosses his thwackers aside.

The person who is thwacked becomes a new It, picks up the thwacker, and tries to thwack someone else. Lots of laughter and energy result.

EQUIPMENT

_ 5 or more thwackers
_ A large open area

SAFETY
Be sure the playing area is free of tripping hazards.

[95] A thwacker is a 4- to 8-foot length of pipe insulation tubing, also known as a boffer or a noodle. Use thwackers for any tag game.

[96] Or the same number of volunteers as there are thwackers.

TOUCH BLUE[97]

People in a large group often need to have a way to connect with a few others. This activity creates opportunities by having them locate items people have on them, touch the items, and introduce themselves to the person with the item.

Generate a list of items people might be wearing or have on them that are touchable.[98] For example, Touch Blue would require your group members to find people who are wearing something blue, maybe blue jeans, a hat with a blue bill, or socks with blue stripes. You can be creative by including ideas such as "Touch a blue cell phone."

Call out items one at a time. All the participants find someone wearing a blue cap and touch the cap. Give them a moment to introduce themselves to each other, and then start the next round.

EQUIPMENT
_ A list of items to call out

PERSONAL NOTES AND RE-VIEW

---

[97] Touch Blue is just an example. You can call this activity anything you want.

[98] Be sure you don't get too invasive. "Touch a tooth filling" or "touch a bra" are out of line. The items on the list don't strictly have be touchable themselves. You might include hobbies (soda can collecting), interests (astronomy), preferences (opera), and experiences (born in October), too.

MR. HOME APPLIANCE

This activity allows large groups to be active and creative.

Divide into groups of 25 or so. Give them one minute to agree on their favorite home appliance. If you want to make sure groups don't choose the same appliance, you can assign each group a room: kitchen, bathroom, garage, laundry room, living-room.

Once they've decided on the appliance, ask them to create a human sculpture of that appliance using everyone in the group. The sculpture needs to be a working model with moving parts. Give them about ten minutes to create the appliance and practice.

Have each group perform and have the other groups guess what it's supposed to be. You'll be amazed at the creative appliances.

EQUIPMENT
None

PERSONAL NOTES AND RE-VIEW

PERSONAL SCAVENGER HUNT

This activity is a fun way for people to interact that's different than usual. Before the activity generate a list of items they need to collect based on what people may have with them. Here's a sample list:

2002 quarter
Runner with 6 shirts on
Picture of a family pet
7 shoes tied together
$1.38 in change
A mom on the phone (who has to speak with the judge)
Runner with 5 hats on
Runner wearing all the groups' name tags
8 belts in a chain (bonus for longest chain)
First group to make a 10-person pyramid
Pair of Teva sandals
Runner with a pocketful of grass (collected from a nearby field)
9 socks in a roll
Piece of clothing with a Nike logo
Cell phone that plays "Camptown Races (Do Dah)"

Break the group into teams of about 25. Each team designates one person to be the runner. The runner is the only person allowed to bring items to the judge,[99] who is standing in the middle of all the teams.

Call out an item on the list. The first team to bring that item to the judge gets a point.[100] Allow enough time before calling the next item so the teams can return possessions to their owners.

[99] The judge can be you or anyone else you choose.

[100] This can be a competition where the points matter. (They're free—so why not make it 1,000 or 10,000 points?) Or you can make it like *Whose Line Is It Anyway?* where the points don't matter.

EQUIPMENT

_ The list of items

PERSONAL NOTES AND RE-VIEW

NAME CHA-CHA

Use this activity to divide a large group into smaller teams.

Have the whole group stand in a large circle. Ask for the same number of volunteers as teams you want. These volunteers need to be outgoing and loud. The volunteers start in the center of the circle.

Let's say one volunteer is named Antonio. Antonio approaches a person in the circle and asks his name. It's Tim. Antonio performs the Name Cha-Cha, which consists of yelling "Tim" at the top of his lungs in a rhythm: "Tim—Tim—Tim-Tim-Tim" while doing bunny hop footwork.[101]

After Antonio performs the Name Cha-Cha, Tim stands behind him, puts his hands on Antonio's shoulders, and they move across the circle to find someone else. Together they repeat the process. Let's say the next person's name is Cindy. Tim and Antonio perform the Name Cha-Cha together. "Cindy—Cindy—Cindy-Cindy-Cindy."

Tim and Antonio turn around so that Tim is now the leader and Cindy puts her hands on Antonio's shoulders. Tim gets to choose the next person. Each time the line gains a person, they all turn around and put their hands on the shoulders in front of them. The front person is at the back; the back person is now the front and gets to choose the next person.

By the end, everyone is in a group and all the names have been yelled out for everyone to hear.

EQUIPMENT

None

PERSONAL NOTES AND RE-VIEW

[101] Start with feet together. Hop and extend the right foot out (heel down). Hop and extend the left foot out (heel down). Then more quickly, hop and extend the right foot, left foot, and right foot again.

COMPOUND WORD

Have people pair up. Each pair agrees on a compound word or two-word phrase—doghouse, peanut butter, wing nut—and who will say the first part and who will say the second.

Once they've chosen their words, the partners are separated to opposite sides of the field or room. They close their eyes or put on blindfolds. People shout their word and wander around to find their partners.

EQUIPMENT
_ Blindfolds, one for each person (optional)

SAFETY
Since the participants' sight is limited, be careful in choosing the location. Look for hazards. Also be watchful of people walking around, so they don't bump into each other.

PERSONAL NOTES AND RE-VIEW

FIGURE 8

The group forms a Figure 8 with an obstacle (post, chair) in the middle of one of the circles.[102] Have the participants hold hands with the people on their right and left. The goal is to see how many times the group can run through the figure 8 diagram (back to where each person started) in a given amount of time.

Figure 2-10
Figure 8

When you give these basic directions, they'll soon figure out the challenge of dealing with the crossover point.

EQUIPMENT
_ One large obstacle

102 You need the obstacle in the middle to keep the figure 8 form. Without it, the figure degenerates into a simple circle and the crossover challenge is lost.

STAND UP

The activity begins with everyone sitting alone on the ground. Have them all stand up without letting their hands or arms touch the ground.

During the next round everyone finds a partner, and they sit on the ground together. They must stay in contact with each other as they are standing up—the whole time.

Each pair finds another pair, and the four of them must stand up while keeping everyone in contact. Continue combining groups until everyone is standing up together.

EQUIPMENT

None

PERSONAL NOTES AND RE-VIEW

LAP SIT

This is an oldie—but whenever a large group is gathered, you have a great opportunity to try for a record. The group stands in a tight circle all facing the same direction. The tighter the circle, the more likely they'll succeed.

Instruct them to sit down on the lap behind them, everyone at the same time. It helps if you give them a count of three. On "one," they bend their knees. On "two," they touch the knees of the person behind them with their behinds. On "three," they put all their weight on the knees of the person behind them.

If they accomplish this, have them walk while sitting on each other's laps.

EQUIPMENT

None

PERSONAL NOTES AND RE-VIEW

ONE-ON-ONE TAG

Link Tag, TV Tag, Freeze Tag—you remember the endless variations of this simple childhood game. These are great for adults as well, to get them moving around and open to more fun.

1. Have each person find a partner.
2. Decide which of the two will be It. Rock, Paper, Scissors works well for this.
3. People only chase their own partner. All pairs are chasing at the same time. When a person is tagged, she's the new It. She spins around three times before she starts to chase her partner.

EQUIPMENT

None

SAFETY

Discourage full-contact tag. Go around others not through them. If indoors, add walking as a rule; heels must hit the floor first. This is a high-energy game. The group will get tired quickly, so keep boundaries small and the duration short.

PERSONAL NOTES AND RE-VIEW

AMOEBA TAG

One person starts off as It. When It tags someone, the two of them link together by holding hands or linking elbows, and the chase continues. Each person tagged joins the amoeba until everyone is caught.

EQUIPMENT

None

PERSONAL NOTES AND RE-VIEW

Planning Exercises

Planning a meeting, event, or retreat from scratch can be intimidating. A little structure can help overcome the creative block that may accompany a blank page or an empty schedule. The following exercises will assist you in the planning process.[103] All you need for each exercise is paper or index cards and pens. You may also want tape or push pins to post butcher paper or cards on the wall.

These exercises aren't written in stone. Try them out and change them to fit your specific planning needs. You'll find they can be used in many situations.

Goals and Ground Rules

Allowing students to have some influence over what happens during an activity encourages them to get involved. Try this exercise for the first meeting of a small group or at the beginning of a retreat.

Goals

Ask the group to imagine that they've already reached the end of the group's event.[104] It went perfectly. Now they're looking back just before they move on. From that point in the future, how do they expect to answer these questions:

• What happened during the activity?
• How are you different now?
• What did you learn?

After they've had a few minutes to think about those questions, give the group a large sheet of butcher paper and some markers. Let them discuss their answers. They can only write down the ideas they all agree on. The resulting list is the target for them to shoot at—the group goals for the event.

Ground Rules

The idea of ground rules comes from the origins of baseball. When baseball was get-

[103] You'll understand these exercises even better after reviewing Section Three, Program Templates.

[104] Sometimes called *the process* in experiential learning, meaning the group's program, event, or retreat.

ting its start, many small towns had their own teams and their own fields, but there were no standards. Before a game started, the two teams gathered around home plate and discussed how certain situations would be handled—the ground rules. What happens if the ball bounces off the red barn? If the ball goes into the bullpen, it's an out, but if it goes over the pen, it's a home run. The teams would talk about and agree on the rules for the grounds on that day. You can use the same process to get a small group to agree on how to treat each other.

Give them another sheet of paper. Ask them what they need from each other in order to accomplish the goals they've already agreed on. How should they treat each other and what lines need to be drawn for the group and all its members to be successful and safe? Every group member needs to agree on the items that make the list.

Be sure the ideas are specific. If they say teamwork is important, ask them what that means. What does teamwork look like? Have them give examples of what they mean so they have a shared concept of all the ground rules. Once they have a list they think is complete and agreeable to all of them, ask them to sign the ground rules page as an indication that they agree to follow those rules and keep each other accountable to them.

It's also a good idea to give them the freedom to return to the list if they ever feel that the ground rules aren't working. They need to have the freedom to delete, add to, or clarify the list if the whole group agrees that it's needed.

Post the goals and ground rules in a visible place. Occasionally return to them for a quick review to see how things are going. It's a great way for groups to keep focused and to mark progress.

PERSONAL NOTES AND RE-VIEW

BRAINSTORMING

Generating ideas around a specific topic or theme is helpful to any planning process. A bit of structure and some focus make creativity plentiful and useful. Lay a large piece of butcher paper on the floor or table or post it on a smooth wall where everyone can see. If your group is large, you may want to use several pieces of paper. In the center of the paper, write the topic you'll be brainstorming about.

Before you begin, make sure everyone understands the rules for brainstorming.[105]

"If you want to have a good idea, have lots of ideas".

—THOMAS EDISON

RULES OF BRAINSTORMING

• Our objective is *creative* thinking. (We'll do critical thinking later.)
• We're after quantity not quality (at this time).
• We encourage crazy, strange, and wild ideas.
• We allow piggybacking (an original idea springing from a previous idea).
• We allow plussing (adding to another idea).
• We don't allow blocking (shutting down others' ideas).
• We don't allow wimping (withholding your own thoughts or ideas).

It's important to stress that this is the time for creative thinking and not evaluation. Assure the group members that critical thinking and evaluation will come later. Here are a few other ideas to keep in mind when brainstorming:

• Make sure everyone in the group has easy access to paper and pens.
• The goal is to fill the page with ideas.[106]
• Some of the best ideas come near the end of this activity. When you think you've finished, ask, "What else?"

PERSONAL NOTES AND RE-VIEW

CARDSTORMING

Cardstorming follows the rules of brainstorming outlined in the previous section, but the group writes their creative ideas on index cards. Using index cards creates a slightly different dynamic and makes using the results easier. This is also a time for creative thinking, not evaluation, which will come later.

A few things to remember about cardstorming:

• Make sure each person in the group has a stack of index cards and a pen.
• Set a time limit for each concept (optional).

[105] These rules are based on McNair's rules for brainstorming.

[106] Filling up the paper rather than setting a time limit encourages people to look past the obvious ideas to get to the wild ones. I use both time limits and filling up space as guidelines depending on where the group is in the creative process.

• Deal with only one cardstorming concept at a time.
• Write as many different exercises and activities as possible.
• Toss the cards into a pile in the center of the group.

PERSONAL NOTES AND RE-VIEW

CIRCLE, UNDERLINE, OR CROSS OUT

Once you've allowed yourself to be creative, it's time to use your critical thinking skills. Use this exercise to make your brainstorming useful. Identify each idea from your brainstormed list as being connected, neutral, or negative. Circle the ideas that are most closely connected to the topic, underline the ideas that are neutral,[107] and cross out the ideas that are negative or distracting.

If you did cardstorming instead of brainstorming, spread the cards all over a table. Circle, underline, and cross out the ideas on each card. Place the cards into piles after you have finished evaluating all the ideas.

Either way, the result is a manageable list of ideas that are focused directly on your original topic.

PERSONAL NOTES AND RE-VIEW

[107] Neutral ideas are ones that may not be directly related to the topic but are not distracting or counter to it.

CLUMPING

An alternative to Circle, Underline, or Cross Out (above) is Clumping. This process also helps you move from creativity to practicality.

Assign one person to be the secretary, scribe, or keeper of the pen.

Clump ideas into related groups. Which are similar? Are any so closely related as to be indistinguishable? Attempt to reach consensus when clumping.

Don't attempt to designate titles or categories for the clumps until the end of this activity. Groups may want to define the clumps before they even begin the process. If they wait until later, they may find different or new categories than they first imagined.

Discuss relationships before writing down the connections. The scribe circles and connects related ideas on the page and labels them later on. If the group is using index cards, they can move the cards around into different piles.

PERSONAL NOTES AND RE-VIEW

PLATONIC TRIANGLE

If every idea is important, it's difficult to make decisions and use resources effectively. Use this exercise to determine the relative importance of a set of ideas or activities.[108] The *process* is as important as the *product*.

Draw a triangle on a large piece of butcher paper. Create boxes along the base so you have one for each idea you're considering. Place the paper where everyone can see it.

Write one component concept (individual idea) in each box along the base of the triangle.

Just above the first row of boxes, draw another row of boxes—but one less than in the first row. Discuss which concepts to move up and which one will not advance. Work toward consensus. Continue this process until only one concept remains when you get to the top of the triangle.

Work from the bottom up. *Do not* go directly to the top.

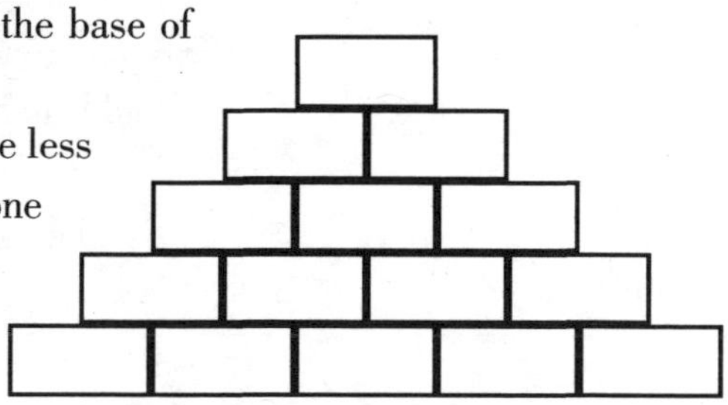

PERSONAL NOTES AND RE-VIEW

Figure 2-11
Platonic Triangle

[108] For example, a group making budget decisions or a group planning a camp would benefit from this activity.

BUILD A CARD PROGRAM

Once you've done brainstorming and grouping exercises, set one pile of ideas in the middle of the group. (If they aren't already, jot them on cards or make adjustments.) Allow a brief question-and-answer time to explain unfamiliar activities and how they relate to the concept.

Create a continuum of ideas from most applicable to least applicable. Discuss each card; place it in relationship to the others from most relevant to least. Once the group reaches agreement on an idea, move on to the next component concept.

Move cards around into different configurations. Discuss the pros and cons of the changes. Continue editing until a quality sequence presents itself. Transcribe card program onto pages for final evaluation.

Save all the cards, whether used or not, for the future.

PERSONAL NOTES AND RE-VIEW

CHOOSING THE BASICS

Whenever you begin a project, decide on the basics first. Write out answers to the following questions:

- **Who?** Who are you planning this event for? You may be targeting the entire youth group, eighth graders only, or a broader group such as students and their friends.
- **Why?** What's the point of this event? Recreation, community service, education, and worship are a few possibilities.
- **What?** What do you plan to do? What is the main activity you're going to wrap the day around?
- **Where?** Where will you be holding the event? Will it take place on your church campus or at another location? Take into consideration factors such as travel time and transportation.
- **When?** On what date and at what time will this event take place? Check to see whether other events or circumstances—holidays, sporting events, church programs, finals—might impact participation.
- **How?** How long will the event last? How much will it cost? Is there a limit to how many students can go?

These are the most basic questions you can ask. Start with any of them, but answer all of them.

THE PRAXIS LENS

Remember that a model of theory is like a lens. Look through it to make your planning clearer. The Praxis lens is a great assessment tool, so take time to look at your ministry through it.[109] What models and theories of ministry are you familiar with? Have you selected one purposefully? Are you keeping up with the latest media developments and recreational trends so they can be used appropriately? Are you giving students and staff the time and space to wrestle with their calling and encouraging them to own it?

List all the components of your ministry. Label each one with a T for theory, A for action, or R for reflection. You may be tempted to assign more than one function to some components, but determine which is primary and use that one.

When you're finished, look over the results. What do you notice? What new connections do you can see? How might you use these parts of your ministry more intentionally?

Look at your ministry components in a different way. Make three columns on a new piece of paper. Label the columns theory, action, and reflection. Write each ministry in the appropriate column.

COMPONENTS OF OUR MINISTRY	
Sunday lesson	**T**
Worship time	**A**
Visit retirement home	**A**
Midweek Bible study	**T**
Small group discussion	**R**
Accountability groups	**A**
Student journals	**R**
Mexico mission trip	**A**

MINISTRY BY FUNCTION		
THEORY	**ACTION**	**REFLECTION**
Sunday Lesson	Worship Time	Small Group Discussion
Midweek Bible Study	Visit Retirement Home	Student Journals
	Accountability Groups	
	Mexico Missions Trip	

Which list is longest? Which is shortest? This chart will give a sense of what you're most comfortable with and where you might want to add effort.

Praxis is a great assessment tool, but it's also a great way to look at programming and event planning. As you begin to plan a program, intentionally anchor it to a model or theory. Allow the wisdom of others to give you a head start. Be sure to

[109] To review, see page 18.

let your leadership and staff know what you're attempting and why you think it will work. Also remember that there are no throwaway moments in ministry. Even if the event is pure recreation, ask yourself, "What lessons might students be learning by attending this event?" These are all theory questions.

Next ask yourself what's going to happen at the event. What will students do and what will staff do to make it happen? Use the model you have chosen to see if an activity fits into your plan. If an activity doesn't help bring you closer to your desired outcome, don't use it. But if it does, hold on to it until you find one that might work better. If an activity is neutral, ask yourself if it's worth the time and resources required to pull it off. Also see if any tools already exist that will make your job easier. Other ministries may have already created sign-up forms, release forms, props and decorations, or crowd breakers. Borrow these and adapt them to your program. These are the action questions.

The reflection aspect isn't as straightforward as theory and action. Can you build open space into the program? Do students have time to wrestle with the content or with their own experience? A few minutes of silence before and after a discussion works or offer an opportunity for journal writing. Artistic activities such as sculpting, drawing, and origami[110] attached to the experience will give students a chance to allow the total experience to impact them. This reflection encourages them to get beyond the question of whether they had a good time to how their lives might be changed.

PERSONAL NOTES AND RE-VIEW

FINDING THE LOOPINESS

To improve your program planning, use the Amazing Learning Loop of Depth (see page 22) intentionally with these steps.

List at all the components of the program you're planning. Then on a blank piece of paper, write four headings across the top: inform, apply, reflect, re-view. Look for the loopiness factor in each component and write it under the heading it best fits. Some ideas may fit under two or three headings. That's okay. List the same idea multiple times. For example singing can fit under Apply and Reflect.

---

[110] Yes I said origami. The ancient art of paper folding.

Figure 2-12
Finding the Loopiness Chart

INFORM	APPLY	REFLECT	REVIEW

Once all the ideas have been transferred to the list, set it down and take a deep breath. Look at this new chart. What jumps out? What connections do you notice?[111] Which ideas seem to make a natural loop? Is there an obvious starting point or ending point? Is there the potential for more than one loop from this list?

A yes answer to any of these questions make the rest of your planning a snap. If nothing stands out, you'll need to choose a series of ideas that will create a learning loop. While many people naturally start a learning loop at *inform*, any part of the learning loop is a valid place to start.

It's a good idea to write out loops in the form of a flow chart to get a better understanding of how the meeting or event might work.

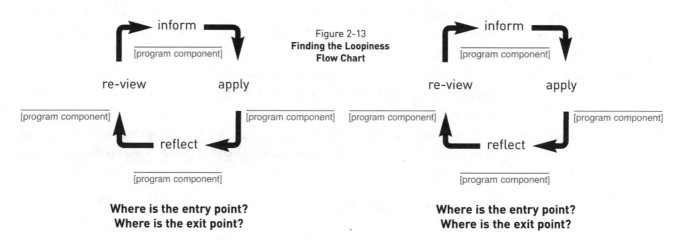

Figure 2-13
Finding the Loopiness Flow Chart

Where is the entry point?
Where is the exit point?

(The exit point of one loop connects to the entry point of the next loop.)

If your list lends itself to more than one learning loop, evaluate the time elements. Given the time each portion of the loop needs, is there enough time to do them all and do them well in one meeting? If you have more loops than fit into one meeting, present the topic over several meetings or reduce the content you intend to present.

You'll find an example in Appendix A (page 148).

111 Remember when you used to take matching tests by drawing lines between terms and their definitions or explanations? In a similar way, try drawing a line from one idea to another to another in ways that flow naturally.

FUN WITH LOGISTICS

At some point early in the planning stage, you need to think through which people need to know what information. Who are the interested players? Take a few minutes to brainstorm all the groups or individuals who'll be involved in pulling off this event: students, parents, church leaders (your boss), staff, volunteers, venders (amusement park personnel, performers, artists, speakers) These people all need to have some information.

Now, by a series of mini brainstorms, ask yourself two questions about each player:

• What questions might this person or group have?
• What information does this person or group need?

For example, parents might ask who will be at the event, what people will be doing there, when the event is scheduled (date, drop off and pick up time), and how much it will cost. These are all things they need to know.

If you hire a speaker, he needs different information, such as when he needs to show up, how long he has to speak, what the focus of the event is, and how much the honorarium is.

The more questions you anticipate, the better your planning will be. The answers will be essential as you create informational tools, sign-up forms, permission forms, and so on.

PERSONAL NOTES AND RE-VIEW

MORE FUN WITH LOGISTICS

You'll also need to plan the logistics for the program as well. Once you have a good idea of what your program will be, you'll have to figure out how to make it happen.

If you haven't already done it, create a tentative schedule. Be sure to include all the meals, meetings, special events, and other activities in this schedule. Ask three questions about each component of your schedule:

• What needs to be done to make this happen?
• What equipment is needed?
• Who's going to be responsible for gathering the equipment and making this part of the program happen?

Involving staff or volunteers can make this process more fun and effective. Invite some of your key leaders to lunch or dinner and talk about these questions. From these conversations generate an equipment list and task list for each part of the program.

Listen to your leaders as you make the schedule and create your equipment and task lists. Listen for who has energy or expertise in any of the areas. As you plan, you'll find someone excited about one aspect of the program and other people excited about other components. Try to match passions and gifts with corresponding tasks. You may not be able to make perfect matches every time, but this is a good way to start delegating. Make sure one person is in charge of each part of the program. She may not actually do everything on her task list herself, but she needs to make sure everything for her activity is done.

PERSONAL NOTES AND RE-VIEW

STEPPING STONES

Stepping Stones helps you flesh out transitions from one concept, idea, or location to another. Write the starting point on one card and where you want to end up on another. Using Cardstorming, write as many possible connections as you can think of on separate index cards. Take all the cards and explore as many possible sequences as you can. Which one makes the most sense?

Instead of using index cards, you can go through the same process on a single sheet of paper using a diagram like one of these (now called Creative Connections):

Figure 2-14
Creative Connections 1

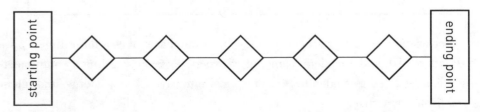

Write one connection in each diamond (though you don't have to use them all or you can add more).

Figure 2-15
Creative Connections 2

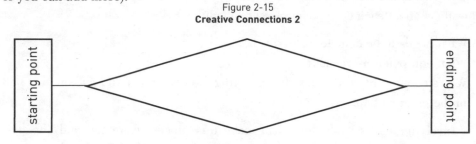

Use this diagram if you don't want the constraints of individual spaces. Write the connections in the space between the starting and ending points.

PERSONAL NOTES AND RE-VIEW

TASK TRACKER

Task Tracker is a tool that gives direction to the delegation process. It's a simple way to evaluate the qualities needed to accomplish a task.

At the top of a blank piece of paper, write four headings: task, time, energy, and expertise. Write down one of the tasks from your to-do list or a job description in the first column. Using a simple rating system (such as ↑, ↓, and ↔), evaluate the task by how much time it should take, how much effort is involved, and how much expertise is required.

Figure 2-16
Task Tracker

TASK	TIME	ENERGY	EXPERTISE
enter student names in database	↑	↓	↔
lead a youth meeting	↔	↑	↑

For example, entering student names into a database takes a lot of time (↑), a little effort (↓), and a moderate amount of expertise (↔). Leading a youth meeting might be rated as moderate (↔) for time, intensive (↑) for energy, and intensive (↑) for expertise.

Repeat the process with other tasks. Use the results of Task Tracker to make delegation easy and effective, since you can more easily match individuals' skills, training, and experience with the tasks that need to get done. You can also use the results to create accurate and effective job descriptions for staff. Tasks that require less expertise and more time or effort can be shifted toward entry-level positions, and those that require more expertise can be shifted to people with more experience. Another application for Task Tracker results is designing internships.[112]

PERSONAL NOTES AND RE-VIEW

A CREATIVE PROCESS
Here's one example of how you can link several of the exercises together to develop a usable program.

1. Brainstorm component concepts for the topic on butcher paper.
   What concepts do people need to grasp in order to understand the topic?

2. Clump the concepts into related groups.
   Which ideas are similar? Are any so closely related as to be indistinguishable?

3. Evaluate and prioritize component ideas using the Platonic Triangle.
   Which ideas are most critical to the understanding of the topic? Which ideas are dependent on each other? Does one idea need to be sequenced before another? Which concepts will you address during your program?

4. Use Cardstorming to develop possible activities and exercises for each of the chosen component concepts you will offer during the program.
   Cardstorm for a set amount of time on one component. When the time limit is up, move on to the next component and repeat the process until you have addressed them all.

5. Use Build a Card Program to evaluate the card piles—one component concept at a time—for applicability and practicality.

[112] See Internship Template on page 147.

Which activities best fit the concepts and resources available? Edit concepts and activities for logical, progressive sequencing and realistic time constraints.

PERSONAL NOTES AND RE-VIEW

Section Three

Program Templates

Program Templates

Do you know what a Spirograph is? This toy was one of my favorites as a child. It came with a rectangular and a circular frame, several round disks, paper, and colored ballpoint pens. The frames had teeth on the edges like machine gears. The disks had teeth on the edges and holes in the middle. The holes were just big enough to stick a pen into.

I would secure one of the frames onto a piece of blank paper and lay a disk inside the frame, meshing the teeth together. When I placed a pen into one of the holes in the disk and pushed it around the frame, I created a beautiful, elaborate pattern. The cool part was when I moved the pen to a different hole in the same disk, I created a completely new, unique design. Same disk, new variables, different design.

The templates[113] I offer in this section work in much the same way as the Spirograph. I'm giving you a frame and a disk. You chose the color of the pen and the hole to put it in. Switch around a few components, use different activities, change the sequence, or move the location to create whole new programs, all while using the same template.

These templates offer a general format or some guiding questions that will help you understand how to use experiential methods in different ministry settings. The usefulness of each template is limited only by your imagination. I've given you samples in Appendix A (page 148) to paint more specific pictures of what the templates might look like when you put them to use.

By exploring the templates you may also gain a deeper understanding of experiential methods. The more you experiment with the templates and find out how they actually work, the more you will understand how to intentionally use experience in that area of ministry. Through your own experiences, you'll create your own methods and applications. Eventually the templates will become irrelevant. Through your successes and failures, you'll gain your own authority and voice and will be able to break new ground.

In this section you'll find five templates, one for each of the most common min-

113 I use *templates* for lack of a better term. They might also be called *frameworks*, or *general formats*. Whatever they're called, these are planning sequences that result in the powerful application of experiential methods.

istry situations: youth meetings, accountability or small groups, full-day events, retreats and camps, and internships. You'll find samples of the templates in Appendix A (page 148).

Youth Meetings

Whether it's Sunday morning or Wednesday night, youth meetings form the backbone of many youth ministries. All the students gather in one place to learn about God and to hang out with each other. Games, worship, and refreshments are often part of this meeting time. Some people call this meeting Sunday school[114] or the midweek Bible study. Other groups come up with catchy names like Shock Wave or Impact. Whatever it's called or whenever it's held, the intentional use of experiential methods can increase its power and effectiveness in touching the lives of students.

Youth meetings look and feel different from ministry to ministry. A small youth group in the inner city has different needs than a megagroup in the suburbs. Group size, location, and resources vary from group to group, but the reasons the group is brought together in a youth meeting format are similar.[115]

For this template, let's assume the main goals of the youth meeting are to teach and to have fellowship. We'll also assume these meetings happen on a regular basis and are open to anyone who wants to come. While there may be opportunities to break into small groups for discussion, this meeting focuses on the whole group. Let's take a look at how experiential methods might be used with these parameters.

Start with the End

Before you choose activities, games, or songs, ask yourself the most basic question: What's the main point of *this* meeting? You want your students to learn about God and fellowship at all youth meetings, but what do you want to happen because of this *particular* program?

To start with the end means you first decide, in general terms, what you want the students to be thinking, saying, or doing when they walk away from the meeting. By deciding the overall main point of the meeting early, you create a decision-making tool. If an activity doesn't support the main point of the meeting, then you know not to use it at this particular time. If a song or game helps make the point or is neu-

[114] Especially if it happens on a Sunday morning.

[115] If you haven't taken the time to ask yourself about the reasons or goals behind your meeting times, it's a good idea to invest the time in that.

tral, then keep it as a possible component of the program.

Remember there are no throwaway moments in ministry. Don't waste your time or resources with activities that don't move people toward your objective—which ultimately is growth.

What makes for a good main point? *Love* is a great topic but may be too big to cover in one meeting. What specifically about love do you want your students to to know or to wrestle with when this meeting is over? More specific topics are loving your enemy, the three kinds of love,[116] and love's role in dating and sex. These will be more helpful when you're trying to decide what Scripture, songs, and activities to include in your meeting.

If you're going through a book of the Bible, you'll still need to make decisions. First you need to decide how much Scripture to cover in one meeting. One verse may not provide enough material to wrap a whole meeting around, but you may not be able to do justice to a whole chapter.

Even with small portions of Scripture you may have to choose from a number of important lessons. The richness of Matthew 5:3-12[117] presents a challenge. Do you focus the lesson on the concept of blessings, Jesus' teaching about applying external laws to internal attitudes, or the radical, countercultural nature of Jesus' words? You may even decide to teach an overview, but you still have to choose something.

Choosing a good main point that's broad enough to be interesting yet still helps you focus your decisions will make the rest of your meeting planning a breeze.

Shoot for a Loop

How will it help you to have a good main point? Let's say you've decided the point of the meeting is Life Together: The Church as a Body. This is a great topic rich with potential.[118] Take some time to exercise your imagination. With your staff or on your own, brainstorm[119] on this topic. Write the main point, Life Together: The Church as a Body, in the middle of a large piece of butcher paper. Fill up the paper with ideas of Scripture, songs, games, decorations, activities, and anything else that comes to mind around the main point.

Your brainstorming session should result in a huge volume of possible content for your meeting. The ideas might range from singing "We Are the Family of God" to playing the game Mr. Home Appliance.[120]

Once you've allowed yourself to be creative, it's time to use your critical thinking skills with Circle, Underline, or Cross Out.[121] Based on the main point, categorize each idea. Circle the ideas that most help you make the main point, underline the ideas that are neutral, and cross out the ideas that are negative or distracting. You end up with more activities than you could possibly do in one meeting, and each one is directly related to the main point.

Now is the time to make use of The Amazing Learning Loop of Depth. On a blank piece of paper write four headings across the top: inform, apply, reflect, review. Look for the loopiness factor of each idea.[122] Transfer the ideas you circled or underlined to this new paper, placing each idea under the heading it fits into best. Some may fit under two or three headings. That's okay. Write the idea in each cate-

116 Eros, phileo, and agape.

117 The Beatitudes.

118 In fact I think this topic deserves a series of meetings to itself. But I'm extremely biased about this topic.

119 See Brainstorming on page 104.

120 Mr. Home Appliance is found on page 96.

121 Circle, Underline, or Cross Out is on page 106.

122 See Finding the Loopiness on page 110.

gory.

Once all the ideas have been transferred to the loopiness chart, look for natural connections for one or more loops. You can start the learning loop at any point, not only *inform*. Now write out the loops in a flow chart[123] to better understand how the meeting might work.

Give Them a Reason to Return

The last part of the youth meetings template is what might be called *the hook* or the *stickiness factor*. What will get the students to live out the lesson and come back for the next meeting?

Ultimately the hook needs to connect the current meeting to the next meeting, but it can take several functions and several forms. Functionally the hook can be a review of the current topic, it can preview the next topic, or it can highlight how the two are related. The hook can take the form of a challenge, a question, or a promise.

Let's say you want to review the current topic: Who or what is the thief in John 10:10? You might want to challenge your students to uncover and change something that has been stealing their life from them. If you wanted to connect this topic with the next meeting's topic on Heroes of Hebrews 11, you might ask these questions:

• What did it take to get on this list?
• How is the thief keeping *you* from getting on it?

You could preview the next topic with a promise: At our next meeting a real life hero will be here. For a promise to act effectively as a hook, it must be fairly impressive and you must be able to deliver. Promising punch to drink at the next meeting may not work well, but worse, promising a free steak dinner and not delivering causes damage.

A little creative thinking will help you figure out a good hook, so try Stepping Stones.[124] On two index cards write down the current meeting's main point and the next meeting's main point. On separate cards write down all the possible connections you can think of between these two topics. See how these two topics might connect with as few cards as possible.[125] As you play with these ideas, the function and form emerge.

Youth Meeting Template Summary
Start with the end

• Decide on the main point of the meeting.

Shoot for a loop

• Brainstorm ideas connected to the loop.
• Evaluate ideas based on whether they're helpful, neutral, or negative.
• Rewrite the list using only the helpful and neutral ideas based on where they fit

[123] See Finding the Loopiness Flow Chart on page 110.

[124] See Stepping Stones on page 113.

[125] It's like six degrees of separation, only with ideas instead of people.

in the Amazing Learning Loop of Depth.

• Look for natural loops, starting and ending points, and multiple loops.

• Write out learning loops in a flow chart.

Give them a reason to return

• Do Stepping Stones.

• Decide on the function: review, preview, or connect.

• Decide on the form: challenge, question, or promise.

Check out Appendix A (page 148) for a sample meeting.

Small Groups

Chapter 3.2

Small groups are the current buzz in ministry. The term not only refers to the number of people in a group,[126] it also implies methods and a format that differ from other types of meetings.[127]

In many small ministries this format and method occur naturally and almost unconsciously. In large ministries, small groups have been recognized as a powerful way to generate community and accountability, but they have to be created artificially. This format allows students to break through the anonymity of the crowd so they feel known and cared for. No matter the size of your group, the small group format offers a powerful environment for students to explore what it really means to be a follower of Jesus.

The number of people in a group only partially defines a small group program. For this template we'll assume the size of each small group is between three and 12. But other factors define small groups as well. The group needs to meet on a regular basis[128] for a long time.[129] The group members agree on and are committed to shared goals and assumptions and to regular participation. All these factors work together to create a powerful context in which students explore their relationships with God and each other.

Finding Things to Talk About

Hanging out with a small group of people is great. What's even better is having something to talk about.[130] What's even better than that is sharing a common goal that lends itself to deep conversation, daring challenges, and personal transformation.

Once you decide a small group program fits the needs of your students, you should answer a few basic questions to give direction and purpose to the groups and to help people decide whether they want to join the groups as leaders, as participants, or not at all. Deciding the group's purpose and defining the leader's role align expectations so people know what they're getting into and can fully commit to the

[126] Even though that's what the name implies.

[127] While this book offers insight into making small groups experiential, I recommend looking into resources specifically about small groups as well. (Try *Help! I'm a Small Group Leader!* and *Small Group Qs* from Youth Specialities.)

[128] This section doesn't apply to discussion groups that are formed temporarily during a large group meeting or groups that are reformed every meeting.

[129] "Long period of time" is relative. For this discussion, three months qualifies as a long time.

[130] I've had a few painful small group moments where eyeballs started to dry out because of excessive staring.

group.[131]

Choosing a general purpose helps you plan for a small group program. There are three general formats for small groups: the study group, the accountability group, and the support group.

The study group focuses on a group exploration of a portion of Scripture, a book, or a specific topic. This format encourages students to gain a deeper understanding of God's Word and pushes them to integrate the knowledge gained into their lives.

Accountability groups challenge students to form deep relationships with a few of their peers through which they can share the struggles and triumphs of their lives. Because of the intimacy that's needed for accountability relationships, this format should be limited to three to five students per group.

Support groups form around a common situation or experience. The shared experience of being an athlete or being addicted becomes the driving force of these groups.

Selecting one of these three general purposes for your small group program provides an anchor as you make other vital program choices.

How many students should be in the group? Earlier in this section I defined small groups as consisting of three to 12 people, but that's still a big range. For planning purposes you may want to be more specific. Accountability groups need to be small—three to five people—to create the best environment for that format. You may want to have 10 to 12 people in study groups to increase the number of opinions and perspectives. The size of the group also determines the number of leaders you need to recruit and train.

How often will the group meet? Support groups may meet a few times a week while some accountability groups may meet only once a month or even once a year. Deciding on the frequency of meetings helps people understand how their commitment to the group will impact their schedule. The same is true of the duration of the group.

How long is this group committed to meeting? Although the relationships formed and the personal changes made because of small groups can last a lifetime, it's a good idea to define the length of time that specific groups will meet, perhaps a quarter or semester, perhaps for an entire year.

Who will be a part of the group and how will participants be selected? Support groups tend to be self-selected based on students' situations. You may want to randomly pull names from a hat to form study groups. Or divide by grade, gender, or location. Whatever you choose, decide on the method early.

Where will the small groups meet? Consider whether you have enough room at your church for each of the small groups to have their own space. You may want to have the groups meet in homes or restaurants or other public locations.

As you answer these questions, also ask yourself how each choice affects the others. Don't let these groups form by accident. Experiment with the variables so they best serve the unique needs of your ministry.

The Leader Makes the Difference

One of the most important lessons I've learned about small groups is *the leader*

[131] Choosing the Basics on page 108 helps get to these answers.

makes the difference. The quality of the leaders directly influences the success of your small group ministry. A good leader can make poor curriculum spectacular. On the other hand, great material becomes irrelevant in the hands of a poor leader. The time and resources spent recruiting, training, and supporting your leaders is a good investment.

Almost certainly your small group leaders will be volunteers. As you plan your small group program, keep in mind that the leaders' time is a valuable gift to you. Don't waste it. But be sure to give them skills, resources, and support so they can be successful and effective. Training and support also absorb your volunteers' time.

That creates tension. On the one hand we want to offer leadership training, and the other hand we don't want to ask for too much of our volunteers' time. We fear that if we ask for too much time, we'll never get enough leaders to commit.

What I've discovered is that people are more than willing to volunteer if the expectations and commitment are clearly defined. An amorphous, undefined volunteer role will frighten more people away then a well-defined, time intensive leadership position.[132] If you're clear on the level of commitment you expect, you'll attract the right volunteers and leaders.

How much time will they need to give as a small group leader and how will their time be spent? After giving clear definition to the groups, the next step is to make choices about the kind of commitment you expect from the leaders and what the leaders can expect of you as a coordinator. You need to have at least one leadership meeting before the small groups actually start. You may want to offer additional group training in advance, depending on the purpose and content of the small groups. I recommend support and in-service meetings throughout the duration of the small group program too. As you recruit leaders be sure to inform them of all the time required of them, including actual time with the small group, training before the small group begins, and support or in-service meetings.

Be realistic as you recruit. Don't bait and switch by telling potential leaders it won't take much time and then springing a bunch of unexpected meetings on them. They might quit—or even worse, they might walk away in bitterness. Take the answers to these questions, schedule a few informational meetings and create informational materials to give to potential leaders.

How do I find quality leaders for small groups? To begin with, try to recruit quality people. You may need one or two leaders or 30 or 40. Either way find people who have enough time, energy, and desire to commit to a group of students for a significant amount of time. The right people can be hard to find if you aren't looking in the right places. They seldom walk into your office and offer their services.[133] If you clearly define the task and actively seek volunteers, you'll find that many people are ready and willing. They're waiting to be asked to participate.

Take a few minutes to brainstorm target-rich environments for potential leaders. Many church ministries encourage community service. College groups, men's groups, and women's groups are great places to look for potential leaders. Other sources are universities and parachurch organizations. Your community is unique and with a bit of creative thought you can think of several other places to find leaders.

Once you've identified sources for potential leaders, send everyone you can

[132] Of course this is true only to a point. You won't get many volunteers for a 40-hour-a-week commitment.

[133] I've heard of this happening, but don't count on it.

think of the informational materials you've created. Then look at your list and choose the three most promising sources and set up visits. See if you can schedule times to speak to the groups in person to generate interest in your leadership opportunities and to pass along the times and location of the informational meetings.[134]

At the informational meetings be absolutely clear about what you're asking of volunteers. And ask attenders for a commitment. Aim to have people who are willing to lead a small group committed to the first training meeting (on their calendar) when they walk away from the informational meeting.[135]

What do volunteers need to be successful? After you've recruited an excellent group of people to lead your small groups, you need to offer training or orientation. Ask yourself what skills or information they need before the groups meet. If leaders are directing a study group, they need to be familiar with the curriculum. Support group leaders may require additional training in leading discussions or about specific issues. Using A Creative Process[136] will help you decide on content for training. Here are components that should be part of every small group leadership training:

• A discussion of the purpose and content of the groups.
• How to lead small groups.
• How to guide discussions.
• A description of group processes.
• A general description of the mental, spiritual, emotional, and social development of the students in the group.

How will you care for leaders while they're in the midst of leading their groups? If you expect leaders to continue to give of themselves, make sure they're being fed. Fill their cups rather than draining them. Support or In-service meetings create opportunities for leaders to be fed, to bounce ideas off of peers, or share successes and frustrations.

You're essentially creating a small group for your leaders. They're your small group, and you're their small group leader. All the basic questions of size,[137] frequency, location, and so on need to be addressed for this small group. The purpose is mutual support and leadership skill development. As the coordinator, you're able to stay in touch with the process of each small group. You're able to celebrate important decisions and avoid potential problems with the small group leaders. Meetings like this offer ongoing encouragement for your leaders to keep them energized, and they'll keep you informed about how each small group is progressing.

What happens when the small group leaders come to the end of their commitment? The leaders should be given the opportunity to debrief and to celebrate. This meeting is important for several reasons. Celebrating the end of their commitment is a great way to say thank you and to acknowledge their gift of service. It also creates an official ending, so leaders can look back on the process as a whole experience.

As they reflect and re-view, they'll be able to identify where they've grown as individuals and what lessons they might be able to apply to other parts of their lives.

[134] You may find leaders of other groups resistant to giving you access to their people. Build trust by building friendships with other pastors and leaders in your community.

[135] So what happens if you get too many leaders? It's a good problem to have, but it's still a problem. You can create leadership teams, mentor relationships, or see if any other ministries need small group leaders and send extra leaders to them.

[136] See A Creative Process on page 115. You can also put together your own creative process.

[137] If you have a large number of leaders, you may want to create a leadership-support team that leads these small groups.

They'll discover just how valuable the experience was for them, which means they're more likely to be excited about the possibility of leading another small group in the future or recruiting for the next small group program. The effort you invest into celebrating and debriefing pays off in huge dividends.

Starting Right

As with most programs, the coordinator's role is most intense and involved in the planning stages. Once the basic choices have been made and leaders have been recruited and trained, the coordinator needs to allow leaders and students to own their groups.

The transfer of ownership starts even before the groups begin to meet. Getting leaders involved in promoting and recruiting group members gives leaders responsibility for and authority in their groups. Just as ownership needs to be transferred from the coordinator to the group leaders, the group leaders need to let that happen with the students in their groups. Students need to buy into the concept and feel that the group is theirs. This may take a few sessions to really sink in.

Focus the first meeting or two on group formation rather than content. Purposefully create community during those small group sessions. The first meeting should include an opportunity to impact the goals of the group and create their own ground rules.[138] Kick off the small groups with a sequence of initiatives that encourages the individuals in the group to explore how they interact and communicate with each other. Opportunities like these start the groups off intentionally so that, as the groups continue to meet, the interactions grow in depth and intensity.

The Long Haul

It's important for group leaders to understand that the power of small groups shouldn't be gauged by what happens at any single meeting.[139] Small groups go through a process over time. Each time a group gets together is an important part of that process—but it's only a part. Awareness of your group location in the process and of what generally comes next helps leaders be more effective and helps the the small groups be more powerful.

The first meeting for any small group can be pleasant and polite yet still have a shallow feel. Most group meetings in the initial stages are either very nice or very quiet. Students are figuring out whether the group will allow them to be themselves. In the meantime they play it safe by making safe comments, telling safe jokes, and not revealing much of significance.

It takes some time before students feel comfortable enough to reveal their true selves. Leaders don't need to feel encouraged or discouraged as their group moves through these initial stages, because the dynamics are likely to change. It is important to create a safe environment by encouraging the group members to follow their self-created ground rules and by modeling honest and appropriate interaction for them.

As the group members grow more comfortable with each other, they'll begin to

[138] See Goals and Ground Rules on page 103.

[139] Gaining a basic understanding of Group Process Models is very helpful for this aspect of small group programs. Another topic for another book at another time.

experiment with going deeper. This part can get uncomfortable. Leading a small group gets interesting when members toy with taking discussions to a deeper level. Usually this comes in the form of a controversial comment or unexpected[140] personal revelation. Tension under the surface may be brought into the open, or there may be open conflict and dissension in the group.

Tough times put the group at a crossroads. They can work through the storms or retreat to the safety of the shallow interactions they've been hiding behind in the initial stages of the group.

Group leaders may become discouraged at this point with thoughts such as, *My group members hate each other. I must be a terrible leader.* In reality, this is an exciting time in the life of a group. This tension and conflict are necessary. Students need to know they'll be taken seriously and that they're safe if they reveal themselves.

Leaders need to continue maintaining a safe environment but not downplay the tension. They become the referee so students can learn how to deal with the conflict. If the group handles this storm well, they'll know they can trust and care for one another.

It may take a while—or it may never happen—but getting to the other side of this uncomfortable phase of a group's process is one of the most exciting and rewarding parts of being a small group leader. The students begin to ask hard questions, offer heartfelt advice, and explore real issues. Now the leadership of the group can be shared with all the members.

The leader's role changes dramatically at this stage. Leaders can step back and watch as the students take full ownership of the process. Every once in a while a mature and experienced opinion may be needed to move things forward or to keep things on track, but for the most part the group is self-directed. This is a wonderful experience for the small group leader. You should, however, be aware that new conflicts may come up. With each conflict, there's a risk that it may drive the group back into the shallowness of the initial stages.

Ending well is one more important part of getting the most out of a small group experience. As the group's time together winds down, take the opportunity to mark that ending to increase the power and impact of the entire experience with an intentional closing celebration. Let the group members reflect on their time together and the impact of the experience. They need a time to re-view what they've learned and how they've changed through the group experience. Underscoring the lessons learned helps students use them in the future.

This meeting should be a chance to celebrate the wonderful things that have happened, but it should also be an opportunity for students to mourn the end of the group as well. Even though they may continue to see each other, this group of people meeting in this context will never meet in the same way again. That's a loss. As they look back over the time together, they may even be tearful. That's okay.

A closing experience creates a definite ending—which allows a powerful new beginning. The ending inscribes a period—or an exclamation mark—after the whole experience so that the experience is self-contained. The students know it's okay to move on to the next experience, making the transition smoother.

Ending well is as important as starting well. Leaders need to understand that

[140] Unexpected by the group. But the leader may feel the tension growing.

they can begin the group interactions intentionally and that their groups will go through a certain process over time. With this understanding, they'll be more effective overall. They'll also discover increased energy and a deep excitement about leading small groups.

Small Group Meeting Template Summary

Finding things to talk about

- Define the type of small group program: study group, accountability group, support group
- Do Choosing the Basics on page 108.

Leadership makes the difference

- Define the leader's role.
- Use information gathered from Choosing the Basics.
- Clearly communicate time commitments.
- Create an honest job description.
- Recruit quality leaders.
- Create informational materials.
- Schedule informational meetings.
- Brainstorm target-rich leader environments.
- Send information to everyone.
- Schedule meetings with key organizations.
- Train leaders.
- Do A Creative Process (or your variation of it) for the training topics.
- Decide on what leaders need to know before the groups start.
- Create an ongoing support program.
- Celebrate at the end of the small group program.

Starting right

- Encourage the leaders to take ownership of the groups.
- Have leaders promote the small group program.
- Have leaders help recruit group members.
- Focus the first small group meetings on developing community.
- Get group input on goals and ground rules.
- Design an initiative program for the first session to explore group interaction.

The long haul

- Make sure the leaders know and understand the process of a group.
- Groups begin with shallow interactions.
- Tension develops as the group members go deeper.
- Create an intentional ending experience to give closure to the group.

Full-Day Events

Early in the morning students gather in the parking lot of the church to load onto buses and head out for a day of fun and adventure. They could be on their way to a local amusement park or to work for the day at a retirement home. That evening the buses return[141] full of exhausted students whose minds are filled with precious memories from the day.

Full-day events like these create powerful experiences that impact student's and leader's lives in amazing ways. They're filled with many obvious—and not so obvious—opportunities for learning. With a little creative thinking, the intentional use of experiential methods, and a ton of logistics, full-day events become more than just fun outings. They transform lives.

Full-day events aren't just the extended dance-mix versions of a youth meeting.[142] These programs are *happenings*. They last longer than a regular meeting, but they also need to be something special, something students don't do regularly. These events create an opportunity for your regulars to invite their friends.[143]

Whether the focus is fun or community service, it's the uniqueness of spending most of the day together doing something out of the ordinary that gives this experience power. Due to the uniqueness of these types of events, they tend take more effort to pull off than a Sunday morning or midweek event. Special arrangements such as travel or coordinating with other organizations need to be made. By the end of the day everyone is exhausted. But when you listen to the excitement in your students' voices as they tell their parents and friends about the day, you find it's more than worth the effort.

Who, Why, What, Where, When, How Long, How Much, How Many

Spontaneous road trips with a group of friends are great. Jumping into a car or two and taking off for the day works fine when no one needs to be responsible. But when you're in charge, you need to be organized, because a lot more is at stake.

Being organized isn't just about making sure the kids having fun. It also means being a good steward of money and bringing everyone home safely. Planning and

[141] We hope. Church buses are notorious for breaking down.

[142] Though some poorly planned youth meetings feel like full-day events.

[143] They know some of their friends would never come to Sunday school, but they might go on a beach trip.

administration are not the most exciting parts of ministry, but learning how to plan and administrate well make a huge difference in the effectiveness of your ministry. The secret is that the better you are at these skills, the more time you have for relationships and fun. Not only will your events run smoothly and safely, you'll spend less money and the events will consistently be more successful.

A lot of time, energy, and money are wasted on acting without direction. Many youth workers find it difficult to enjoy the events they plan. The night before a program, they run around until the early morning hours filling last minute needs; the next morning they function on caffeine and adrenaline as they realize they've overlooked important details.

This doesn't need to happen. Thinking through the event early allows you to enjoy the event you planned. The more specific you get in planning, the more you can get done before the day of the event.

Turn back to page 108 and do Choosing the Basics. The questions may seem simplistic or obvious, but missing any of them can bring about big headaches later on. The answers will help you create thorough task lists so that no details slip by unnoticed.

Perhaps you had tickets given to you for Christian Music Day at a local amusement park.[144] That answers the what, when, and where questions, but you still have choices to make about who goes, why you're going, and all of the how questions. Write out answers to the questions and consider the answers carefully to make sure the details work together.

For example if you decide you want to do an event for the high school group, you should check to be sure the date you're planning isn't at the same time as the school's championship football game. If you plan a trip to the beach for a group of 50, you need more than three vans and one driver. Working with the basic questions as you plan your day-long event, helps ensure that you cover the details for a successful and safe event.

Fun with Logistics

By answering the basic questions you create a great foundation for your planning. After answering the basic questions, go back to Fun with Logistics on page 112 and work through that process.

The information you generate is also essential as you create marketing and informational tools and as you develop forms. You'll need flyers, sign-up sheets, waivers or releases, and possibly some other forms. Flyers and sign-up sheets can be made easily given the information you generated through the basic questions and the interested players brainstorms. Mix in some creativity, and you have effective flyers for students, parents, and staff, and you have an efficient sign-up sheet that gives you all the information you need for each student.

Waivers and releases are a different story. These are intended to be legal documents that stand up in court. Your church may already have forms for you to use. If your church doesn't have forms already, you can find examples in *Youth Ministry Management Tools*[145] or on the Internet. Always be sure the waiver and release

144 Beware of "free" stuff. Sometimes free stuff creates more hassles than opportunities. Free tickets may mean that you have to pay for parking, transportation, food, and any number of other unexpected expenses. "Free" can be very expensive.

145 By Ginny Olson, Diane Elliot, and Mike Work (Youth Specialties, 2001).

forms you use are approved by your church's attorney.

The next task is to flesh out the core of the program.[146] Go back to the answers to your why, what, and where questions. From these answers you can figure out what the main focus of the day will be—what event, activity, or program you'll wrap the experience around.

Some events will be more planning intensive than others. If you're taking your students to a local amusement park or to an event sponsored by another organization, you may need only to prepurchase tickets and recruit enough leaders for supervision. However, if you're sponsoring the event or going to lead your own activities at a park, you'll be the one who needs to contact the speaker, arrange for a sound system, and gather all the recreation equipment.

This is a good time to create a tentative schedule for the day. Starting with the time your staff needs to arrive, write down each component of the day with a brief description. After you've completed the schedule, go back over it with your leaders and consider each component individually.[147] Figure out what needs to be done for this part of the day to happen. As you're discussing the schedule, create an equipment list and task list for each component of the day.

If you are planning an adventure day filled with initiatives, one activity may be River Crossing. You would write two ropes and 15 carpet squares on your equipment list. The to-do list might include going to the carpet store to get free carpet samples, going to the hardware store for ropes, and setting up.

If you're planning a lock-in, you may schedule a special speaker. If you haven't decided who will speak, you can make a list of possibilities speakers to invite. You'll need to make sure the speaker knows the topic for the presentation, arrange their transportation to the event, and request the honorarium check so it's ready to hand to the speaker. You might need to add an overhead projector and lapel microphone to your equipment list.

As you develop the schedule and create your equipment and task lists, be ready to delegate. Turn to Task Tracker on page 114 to help with this part of the planning.

You wouldn't know it by reading this book, but I'm not a natural list maker. I've discovered in my years of ministry and event planning that logistics and lists are my friends. The more energy and effort I put into planning an event, the more energy and time I've had to enjoy the event itself. By using lists, I experience fewer surprises, and my mind is free to address the ones that pop up. Good planning provides freedom that is more than worth the effort.

Praxis Applied

The last part of this template involves a quick check to see if all the parts of Praxis are present in the day-long event. Go back to the Praxis Lens on page 109 and evaluate the day you have planned.

You might put an R next to bus ride home and a T next to speaker presentation. You will transfer the day's components onto the second list (ministry by function) with bus ride home under the Reflection column and speaker presentation under the Theory column.

[146] The Fun with Logistics exercise can also be helpful in planning the program

[147] You may have to be a bit more creative if you don't have several staffers or volunteers to do this with. Brainstorming by yourself isn't nearly as fun unless you have multiple personalities. Then it can be entertaining if not really effective.

Once you've transferred all the components, evaluate whether you have any glaring problems. A trip to Disneyland may be heavy on action, but you should have some parts of the day that allow for input and reflection. If you find that you only have components listed under action, go back to the tentative schedule and see what you might add for reflection and theory.

Can you plan a day trip that's all about recreation? Sure. The question is, Why should you? Why pass up an opportunity to intentionally touch a life? Just a word about the importance of laughter or a moment to reflect on being outside can create the space for a student to be transformed.

"We had the experience, but we missed the meaning."

— T.S. ELIOT

Full-Day Event Template Summary

Who, why, what, where, when, how long, how much, how many

• Do Choosing the Basics.

Fun with logistics

• Do Fun with Logistics.
• Create informational flyers and forms.
• Flesh out the program.

Praxis applied

• Evaluate the event with Praxis.

Retreats and Camps

Going to camp changed my life. Like many junior highers, I became a Christian at a campfire in the mountains. I spent my summers during college working at camps and my winters planning and leading retreats and mission trips.[148] Camping has formed much of who I am and how I do ministry.[149]

Taking students out of their routines and placing them in a new environment creates amazing possibilities for transformation. People often refer to mountaintop experiences where they gain clear vision for their lives and walk away with intense energy and drive. They walk back into their every day lives changed and with a passion to impact their communities. Camp programming is all about creating opportunities for God to speak[150] and for us to listen.

Stereo Wars: How Camp Ministry Works

I grew up as the youngest of three brothers. By the time we were all teenagers, we each had our own stereo system and our own taste in music. When I got home from school, I would go to my room and turn on my flip-up portable record player.[151]

I was happy to listen to my music at a reasonable volume until one of my brothers got home. He would go to his room, put on his music and turn up the volume.[152] We lived in a wonderful house but even so, the walls weren't soundproofed. His music would bleed into my room. Not willing to compromise my listening experience, I naturally turned up my stereo so I could hear my music clearly. This increase in volume forced my brother to respond by turning up his music.

The war would end when the noise blasting through the whole house forced our mother to intervene. With the volume and intensity only a mom can achieve, she forced a truce by offering three options: agree on one record or radio station, turn down both stereos to a level that doesn't cause ears to bleed, or lose stereo privileges for the rest of our lives.[153]

Our students have their own stereo war going on. The volume of the world's stereo is turned all the way up. The sound is blaring at school through the media

[148] I include short-term mission experiences in this section as well. If you want to include a trip like this in your ministry, I highly recommend going with an established organization. They have the logistics worked out and know the people and community you'll be working with.

[149] You might be saying, "Ahhh! That's why he likes this experience stuff so much."

[150] Partly by minimizing other voices that compete for our attention.

[151] Yes, these were the days before CD and MP3 players. My music came from 45s or amazing LP technology. The first record I ever bought with my own money was a 45 of "Top of the World" by the Carpenters. (I'm not sure, but I think this purchase may have resulted in a beating from my brothers.)

[152] One of my brothers had an 8-track player. He was convinced it was going to be the next big thing.

[153] Okay. I'm exaggerating a bit. It was usually only a week but to an adolescent losing music privileges for a week seemed like an eternity.

and at home. This wall of noise makes listening to God difficult. When we take them away from home, out of their daily situation, we turn down the world's stereo. We create a space for them to hear a different voice. The way we fill that time, the program we offer, turns up God's stereo. When students are on a retreat, the distractions are reduced and it's easier to hear God's voice.

These types of program have several names: retreats, camps, conferences, service trips. Whatever you call them, they involve going somewhere and spending at least one night away from home. It's important to remember students aren't transferring residence. They end up back home. We're opening up a space by letting them take a break from their daily routines.

Ultimately the purpose of a camp program is to help students take home what they've learned and how they've changed. An overnight retreat or a 10-day backpack trip both act to create the necessary space and open their eyes to the possibility that the world can be more than what they've experienced in their school or community.

Starting Early

Before we go any further in creating a template for retreats and camps,[154] I want to encourage you to take advantage of camping programs that already exist, which will save you a lot of time, energy, and believe it or not, money. It's easy to forget to include the time and energy spent by you and your staff in the final cost of going to camp. Our time is valuable, and the hours spent on logistics and planning can be used in other ways. You'll be freed up to spend time with students instead of shopping for food or building props. Because camps usually present the same program multiple times, they can spend much more money on recreation, decorations, and other program details. While you may have $200 to spend on equipment for games, a camp that does the program 10 times has $2,000 to spend.

One tradeoff is that you have less control over what happens. Find a program you trust so this isn't a problem. Another tradeoff is that your group may share the program with several other churches, although this is more likely to be a benefit. It can be a great experience for your group to meet and mix with others.

Camps and retreats should be a part of every youth ministry. Before you invest in creating your own program, consider the pros and cons of going to a programmed camp.

If you find that planning your own retreat or camp fits your needs, it's essential that you start the process early. Some retreat centers book their facilities a year in advance and even national parks book their campsites eight to 10 months in advance. It's also a good idea to schedule any speakers or special music early. If you're planning a retreat from scratch, I recommend you start the process at least six months out and as much as a year ahead of time.[155]

Before you get too far into planning, create a target to shoot at. That's what Choosing the Basics on page 108 is all about. Do this exercise before you schedule the camp or retreat. Deciding on the foundations and direction early help focus your energy and resources as you move forward with your plans.

[154] Warning! What follows is my opinion.

[155] It's not always possible to begin planning this early. Don't let this stop you from trying. It may be a bit more difficult, and you may not be able to do everything you want, but it's still possible to create a great camp program in less time.

While all the questions in Choosing the Basics are important and the answers to each influence the other questions, you may have to prioritize as you begin to make decisions. What are the most important factors? You may find a location that has a great meeting room and is inexpensive, but if you want this to be a water-ski camp and the site doesn't have a lake, you'll need to find another place. Or you may be getting a great price for a midweek trip, but your students are still in school. The Platonic Triangle on page 107 can help you prioritize these factors so you can see clearly what's important to you and then make good choices.

The location you select will have a huge influence on what you'll be able to do programmatically. Every site is unique. Each has it's own benefits, but they all have limitations as well. If water activities are important to you, choose a location that has a pool or a lake. Check to be sure the location has lots of places to meet if you plan on small group work.

If at all possible, visit the site before you commit to it. Use your imagination as you walk around the grounds. How might the meeting room be set up and decorated? What recreation opportunities does the camp provide? How can you add to them? What unique on-site features can you use in your program?

Take notes and pictures as you walk around. Ask yourself what-if questions: What if we set up a flying disc golf course?[156] What if we brought up sand and palm trees and turned the dining room into a tropical island? Dream big as you walk, but remind yourself that no sight will be perfect. Choose the one that comes closest to your vision and work with it.

Creating Anchors

Once you've answered all the basic questions and decided on a location, you can begin to build the program. This process should start early as well. The more time you give yourself to gather resources and complete tasks, the better your program will be. You don't have to have the program set in stone a month early, but you should be exploring what's possible and making to-do lists six weeks ahead of time.

Creating anchors—things that keep us from drifting—for your retreat increases the impact of the program and makes the overall experience more enjoyable for everyone. In the craziness of the moment, having something that keeps us attached to the original goals is helpful.

A meeting may be going a little longer than planned. This may be no big deal until you realize that you're eating dinner at 9 p.m. and have to cancel the events scheduled for the evening. Schedules can get out of hand if there isn't something that keeps them on track. Meals are great schedule anchors. If you know that dinner will be hot and ready to eat at 6, you're motivated to be there on time. By making the meal times firm, you can keep on track and get to all the important stuff you have planned.

You need program anchors as well. It's amazing how helpful a good theme can be. It focuses the teaching logically so the power and depth are increased. A theme also makes the recreation and activities memorable. A program anchored to a well-thought-out theme works as a synchronized whole rather than a bunch of random

[156] I just wanted to honor all the non-Frisbee flying discs.

parts that may work against each other.

Finding a good theme is challenging. Use A Creative Process on page 115 (or your variation) to choose the theme and develop coordinating lessons, recreation, decorations, and even meals. You'll probably have more ideas than you can possibly use—a great problem to have.

One more step will take your retreat from good to great. Use Finding the Loopiness on page 110 to be intentional about connecting individual events and activities.

After these two planning exercises, you'll have a good idea of all you'll be doing on your retreat. The next step is to identify the details and execute them. Yes, those lovely logistics move your camp program from a dream to reality.

Fun with Logistics

Like planning a full-day event, the logistics[157] involved in pulling off a retreat or camp is a matter of anticipating the needs and questions of those who will be involved. It's easy to be intimidated by the plethora[158] of details that go into planning a camp or retreat. It seems like a huge bite that you could never fit into your mouth.[159] But when you cut that bite into smaller, mouth-sized bits, you can swallow each one separately. Dividing the logistical challenge into manageable sections and then dealing with them one at a time makes it much less intimidating. It also makes it easier to delegate small portions to staff and volunteers. Divide and conquer.

Return to Fun with Logistics on page 112 and More Fun with Logistics on page 112 to help you create flyers, forms, to-do lists, and equipment lists.

Let me offer one last word of advice on logistics. Some people love the details. They allow themselves to get so excited about the planning and logistics that they forget the goal is ministry to the students. Be sure the program determines the logistics, not the other way around. All the forms, lists, and details are intended to make the program a better experience for the students. Planning for the details is only helpful if it frees you up to love and serve your students, their parents, and your staff.

Retreats and Camps Template Summary

Starting early

- Decide whether you'll join a programmed camp or develop your own.
- Book a location, speaker, and the music early.
- Visit potential sites.
- Do Choosing the Basics.

Creating anchors

- Do A Creative Process.
- Find anchors for your schedule.

[157] *Logistics* is just a scary way of saying you need to figure out what information and resources you'll need and how you'll gather those things.

[158] I can hardly say this word without thinking of *The Three Amigos*.

[159] I'm torn between using the image of a huge hunk of cooked cow for the carnivores or the extra large leaf of lettuce for the vegetarians.

- Find anchors for your program.
- Do Finding the Loopiness.

Fun with logistics

- Do Fun with Logistics to create flyers and forms.
- Create to-do lists and equipment lists.
- Delegate to key leaders.

Internships

A college student whose life was changed through a church youth group wants to explore a career in youth ministry. A youth pastor knows what to do and does it well but needs help as the ministry grows. The church can't afford to hire additional staff. An internship program can bring these two needs together and fill them.

An internship isn't simply cheap labor for the church, and it's not just a low paying job for the intern. An experience like this needs to create an opportunity for the intern to explore the world of full-time ministry. This means that the youth pastor needs to invest time and energy into the intern and that the intern should expect to work hard to learn, not only *what* to do in youth ministry, but why and how.

Hiring an intern doesn't necessarily mean less work for you. What will change is the nature of the work. Energy you would have used to run the junior high program—much of what the intern is doing now—is invested in training and supervising the intern. You now minister to junior highers and young adults.

How is an intern different from a volunteer? When I volunteer, I expect little or nothing in return for my time and effort. I offer myself as a gift to the ministry. An internship creates an expectation for a long-term exchange, involving more than cash. The intern expects to benefit from your wisdom and expertise, so the experience needs to include education or training aspects that happen over time.[160]

If the internship doesn't include education or training, the church gets cheap labor, but the intern is cheated. If the internship includes learning opportunities, but the intern doesn't do much, then the church gets cheated. Many internships end up with a winner and a loser, but it doesn't have to be that way. A well-planned internship can be win-win.

Planning for an internship starts with an important question: Am I willing to commit time and energy to working with interns in addition to my other responsibilities? Creating an internship means creating a new, ongoing commitment to an additional component to your overall ministry. If you're feeling tired, overworked, or frustrated, it's not a good idea to take on an intern.[161]

[160] An internship should last at least a quarter (3 months) but may last as long as a few years.

[161] If you don't intend to give anything of educational value to your intern, then change the name to what it really is: volunteer, cheap labor, or indentured servant.

Now that you have an idea of what you might be getting yourself into, you can choose to pursue it or not, but you'll be making your choice with purpose. Planning for interns should start only after you've made this informed choice.

Front-Load Expectations

For an internship to be a positive experience for both parties, not only do you create expectations but you align them as well. The first part of the task involves reflection and re-view. What can you realistically expect from an intern? What can they realistically expect from you? What tasks can you assign to the intern?

When you hire interns, you're hiring novices who may have a lot of energy but not many skills. You can't expect interns to teach a lesson or program an event on the first day. They'll eventually end up at that point, but they usually can't start there. You can't overwhelm them with tasks or responsibilities.

On the other hand you need to make sure they have enough to do. Having too little to do is just as bad as having too much. You need to be willing to hand over some tasks and responsibilities if you want to keep interns engaged and challenged.

Finding the balance between boredom and burnout—and maintaining it—is an ongoing challenge for everyone working with interns. To get a good idea of what tasks might work for an intern, brainstorm a list of potential tasks for interns.[162,163] List all the things that an intern might possibly do for your ministry.

Once you've done the creative thinking, evaluate the tasks using Task Tracker.[164] In the beginning, interns have lots of time and energy but not much expertise. By the end, their skills are developed to the point that they succeed at tasks demanding much more expertise. Using the information generated from the Task Tracker, you can now make some choices about what you expect from interns and what they might expect from you.

From the start, interns can be expected to perform the tasks that require a low level of expertise and moderate to high amounts of time and energy. These tasks might be considered grunt work, but they also lay a foundation for broader experience. Be clear with potential interns that these tasks will be expected, while also being clear about where the internship is headed.

What will they get from the internship experience? The results of the Task Tracker are helpful for answering this question. Take each task that requires a high amount of expertise and ask what skills or knowledge is required to perform that task well. Leading a small group Bible study requires a high level of expertise. The leader requires some knowledge about how to study Scripture and some skills in leading a discussion. Planning a beach day requires a high level of expertise but a slightly different set of skills and knowledge—administrative skills and knowledge about how the church's systems work. As you look at the high expertise tasks, you'll notice that some knowledge and skills begin to repeat themselves. These become a list of what individuals can expect to gain from an intern experience.[165]

The next step in creating an internship program is using the Task Tracker information to create a job description. A good job description creates and aligns expectations clearly. It's a document both you and the intern can rely on to clear up any

[162] You may want to do this series of exercises even if you don't use interns. It can give you a clearer picture of what it takes to do your job.

[163] See Brainstorming on page 104.

[164] See Task Tracker on page 114.

[165] The list you develop can also help you identify goals for your own professional development.

confusion.

Along with the information generated by brainstorming and Task Tracker, make sure other details are spelled out:

- How much time will interns be expected to commit each week or month?
- How long does the internship last?
- When does the internship begin and end?
- Will interns receive money as an honorarium, stipend, or salary?
- Which expenses are covered and which are not?[166]
- Will interns raise support?

These are not the most enjoyable things to talk about, but the clearer you are in the job description, the easier it is to address these issues from the beginning.

Honor the Expectations

Now that you've created a set of expectations and spelled them out in the job description, it's time to figure out how to honor the expectations.[167] Applying the Praxis lens to your task list is helpful at this point. Action is easy to identify; there's always plenty for an intern to do. Deciding on what theory to include and creating opportunities for reflection are a bit more difficult.

If you've done Task Tracker and evaluated the high expertise tasks based on skills and knowledge, then most of the evaluation for action and theory is done. You have a list of skills to develop and a list of concepts (knowledge) to pass along.

Your tasks now are to create opportunities to practice the identified ministry skills, decide how to pass along the knowledge, and help interns connect the experience with the content. The Praxis of an internship means that interns are involved in worthwhile tasks, offered valuable knowledge, and given opportunity for honest reflection.

You can pass along the knowledge in discussions and formal teaching times and by using other experts through required reading assignments, seminars, and conventions.[168]

You can't make the connections between content and experience for interns, but you can encourage them toward these connections by offering opportunities for reflection. Requiring them to keep a journal and giving them some reflective assignments offer space for creating connections. Another great way to encourage reflection is to create an intern support group through which they can process the experiences and the knowledge with others who are on similar journeys. If your church is fortunate enough to have several interns, it's easy to form a group. If you only have one intern, work with other churches in your area to create one.[169]

Creating an internship program means you expect interns to learn and grow throughout their time with you. In your job description you have identified what you hope to accomplish. You know where you want them to end up. Now you need to create a map of how to get there.

Use the skills and knowledge list created on the job description to help you. Review those lists. Do any of the skills depend on other skills? Does a sequence pres-

[166] Will you provide housing? Gas money?

[167] You can take the additional step of giving the intern a chance to negotiate and prioritize the expectations. If you do this, be sure to modify the job description. You and the intern both should sign it.

[168] The Youth Specialties CORE™ and National Youth Worker's Convention are two great opportunities, and I'm not just saying this to score points with my publisher.

[169] See [3.2] Small Groups on page 125 for ideas on creating this type of group.

ent itself naturally? The same goes for the knowledge list. Which topics are the most basic?

Use Stepping Stones on page 113 to help with this process. Write down all the skills listed on the job description on separate index cards; then arrange them in a logical sequence so interns can step from one skill to the next in a logical order of increasing difficulty and responsibility.

Repeat the process with the knowledge list. Arrange the cards in a logical sequence from basic to complex.

The resulting stepping stone paths result in a basic curriculum that creates a sliding scale of responsibility and depth. The program should be designed around the possibility of failure and the probability of success. The tasks and teaching should challenge interns to step out of their comfort zones yet not be so difficult that they crash and burn.[170]

As the internship progresses, comfort zones will expand. Tasks and input should continue to challenge interns throughout the program. This means you continue to increase their levels of responsibility and authority as they gain skills and knowledge.

Once you have the content of the internship placed in a logical sequence, Stepping Stones can also help you create a schedule for the internship program.. Figure out how to make the content fit into the length of the internship.

Finding Interns

All the work you do in planning an internship program makes creating recruiting material easy. More information than you need is already organized. As you create job announcements and flyers, ask yourself what questions interns will ask and what you want them to ask. Be sure to highlight monetary compensation and the valuable skills, knowledge, and experience they'll gain through the internship.

After you've created killer informational materials, you need to get them into the hands of potential interns. Where do these people hang out? Brainstorm potential sources of interns: summer camps, universities, your church's college group. Your community will have other sources as well.

Once you've generated a list, send your information and job announcements to the people and organizations on the list. If possible, schedule visits to key sources so you can talk to groups in person.

Be open to surprises as well. Great interns may be so close you don't recognize them.

Internship programs offer experiences that can expand and strengthen the power of a youth ministry and also increase the effectiveness of the next generation of youth workers. Yet if the program isn't well thought out, it can frustrate both the youth pastor and the intern. By investing the time in planning and by intentionally using experiential models, you can create a program God can use to transform both your students and your interns.

170 The concept of the comfort zone is a great model to explore further, but is yet another topic for another time and another book.

Internship Template Summary

Commit to the internship program

• Assess the time and energy it will take to work with interns and choose it purposefully.

Front-load expectations

• Brainstorm intern tasks.
• Do Task Tracker.
• Create a job description.

Honor the expectations

• Do the Praxis Lens exercise with the results of brainstorming and Task Tracker.
• Create opportunities for reflection, including support groups and journals.
• Do Stepping Stones.

Finding interns

• Create informational materials—announcements and flyers.
• Brainstorm potential sources for interns.
• Distribute the information and meet personally with organizations that may be sources for interns.

Appendix A

Sample Templates

Youth Meetings

YOUTH MEETINGS

Start with the Ending

• Decide on The Point for the meeting - Life Together - The Church as a Body

Shoot for a Loop

• Brainstorm ideas connected to the loop - Not Shown
• Evaluate ideas based on if they are helpful, neutral or negative - Not Shown
• Re-write the list using only the helpful or neutral ideas based on where they fit in the Amazing Learning Loop of Depth
• Look for Natural Loops, Starting and Ending Points and Multiple loops

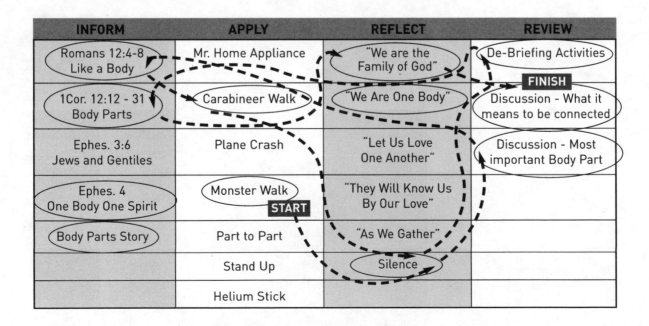

INFORM	APPLY	REFLECT	REVIEW
Romans 12:4-8 Like a Body	Mr. Home Appliance	"We are the Family of God"	De-Briefing Activities
1Cor. 12:12 - 31 Body Parts	Carabineer Walk	"We Are One Body"	**FINISH** Discussion - What it means to be connected
Ephes. 3:6 Jews and Gentiles	Plane Crash	"Let Us Love One Another"	Discussion - Most important Body Part
Ephes. 4 One Body One Spirit	Monster Walk **START**	"They Will Know Us By Our Love"	
Body Parts Story	Part to Part	"As We Gather"	
	Stand Up	Silence	
	Helium Stick		

• Write out learning loops in the form of a flow chart

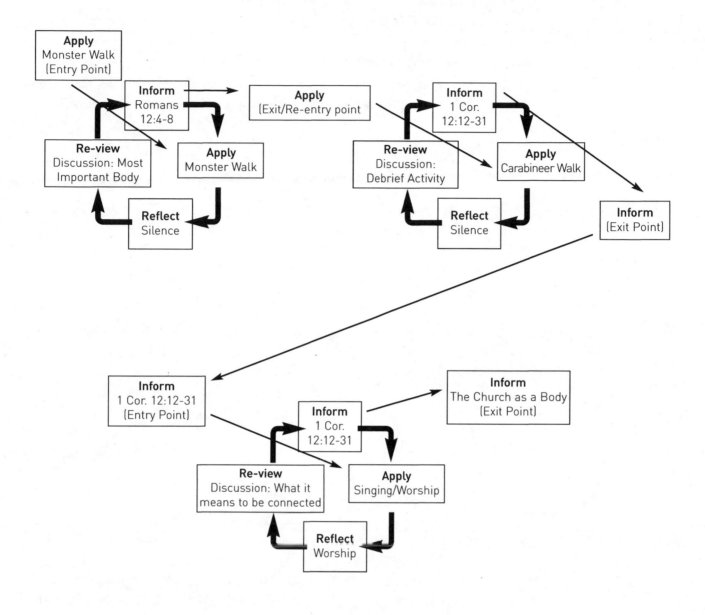

Give them a Reason to Return

• Do the Creative Connections exercise

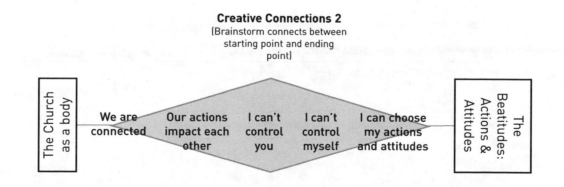

Creative Connections 2
(Brainstorm connects between
starting point and ending
point)

• Decide on Function – Review, Preview or Connect

• Decide on Form – Challenge Question or Promise

The hook will connect the two points with a challenge.

"Between now and next time look for examples of actions and attitudes that help build a better body.   Be ready to tell us about specific examples you witnessed."

Appendix B

The Ultimate Template[171]

This sequence of planning exercises can be used in almost any situation. Each part creates the content for the next. By the end of this process, you'll have a great plan of attack for almost any event, program, or retreat.

Choosing the Basics

Creative Process

Finding the Loopiness or Praxis Lens

Fun with Logistics

More Fun with Logistics

Closing Celebration or Debrief

[171] Generic Template may have been a better title for this, but *ultimate* sounds so much better.

Appendix C

Readings, Resources, and Recommendations

Web Sites

www.adventurehardware.com
Experiential education equipment.

www.adventuresystemsdesigns.com
Leaders in the design, building, and inspection of ropes courses and climbing walls. Includes technical tips.

www.fundoing.com/index.htm
Chris Cavert's site, including activities, training, newsletter, and a store.

www.leahy-inc.com
Equipment, installation hardware, portable teambuilding items, and accessories.

www.teamworkandteamplay.com
Jim Cain's site, including activities, books, and training.

Books

Most of the games and activities in this book are found in or are derived from games and activities in some of these resources. I highly recommend these books for your library.

"There is nothing new under the sun."

—ECCLESIASTES 1:9

Buber, Martin. *I and Thou.* New York: Scribner, 2002.

Cain, Jim and Barry Jolliff. *Teamwork and Teamplay.* Dubuque, Iowa: Kendall/Hunt Publishing, 1998.

Cain, Jim and Tom Smith. *The Book on Racoon Circles.* Tulsa, OK: Learning Unlimited, 2002. (1-888-622-4203)

Dewey, John. *Experience and Education.* New York: Touchstone, 1938.

Fowler, James. *Faith Development and Pastoral Care*, Philadelphia: Fortress Press, 1987.

Frankl, Viktor E. *Man's Search for Meaning*. Boston: Beacon Press, 2000.

Freire, Paulo. *Pedagogy of the Oppressed*. New York: Continuum, 1997.

Kalisch, K.R. *The Role of the Instructor in the Outward Bound Educational Process*. Kearney, NE: Morris Publishing, 1999.

Kolb, D. A. *Experiential Learning*. Englewood Cliffs, NJ: Prentice Hall, 1984.

Nouwen, Henri. *Reaching Out*. Grand Rapids, MI: Zondervan, 1998.

————. *Lifesigns*. New York: Doubleday, 1986.

————. *With Open Hands*. New York: Doubleday, 1986.

Palmer, Parker. *The Active Life*. San Francisco: Jossey-Bass, 1999.

————. *To Know As We Are Known*. San Francisco: Harper SanFrancisco, 1993.

————. *The Courage to Teach*. San Francisco: Jossey-Bass, 1999.

Peterson, Eugene H. *Leap Over a Wall: Earthy Spirituality for Everyday Christians*. San Francisco: Harper Collins, 1997.

Rilke, Rainer Maria. *Letters to a Young Poet*. New York: Norton, 1994.

Rohnke, Karl. *Cowstails and Cobras II*. Dubuque, Iowa: Kendall/Hunt Publishing, 1989.

————. *Silver Bullets*. Dubuque, Iowa: Kendall/Hunt Publishing, 1984.

————. *Bottomless Bag*. Dubuque, Iowa: Kendall/Hunt Publishing, 1991.

Smith, Mark K. "Kurt Lewin: Groups, Experiential Learning and Action Research." In *The Encyclopedia of Informal Education*, 2002. http://www.infed.org/thinkers/et-lewin.htm.

Essential reading

for every member of your youth ministry team, the **Help!** line of resources from YS provides practical tools for surviving and thriving in a variety of youth ministry settings.

Visit our online store to receive quantity discounts!

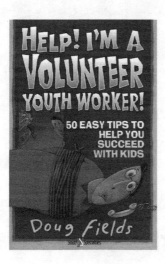

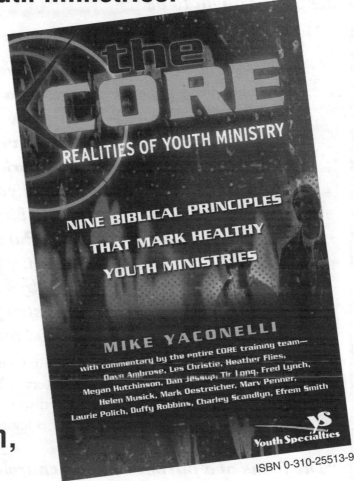

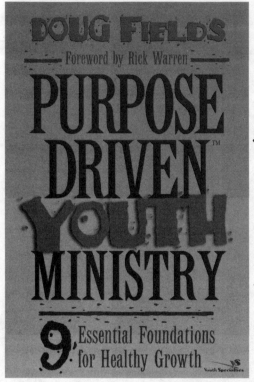